AMERICAN COUNTRY CROSS STITCH

AMERICAN COUNTRY CROSS STITCH

OVER 40 DELIGHTFUL DESIGNS
INSPIRED BY AMERICAN FOLK ART

DOROTHY WOOD

WARD LOCK

ACKNOWLEDGEMENTS

I would like to thank the many people who helped with this publication, using their skills and expertise to produce a really lovely book. Particular thanks are due to Helen Denholm, Crafts Commissioning Editor for her support and encouragement, Richard Carr for the attractive book design, Caroline Hyams, Rosie Anderson and Wendy Hobson for their work on the text and layout, and Paul Bricknall for the excellent photography.

Special thanks go to my husband, David, for his continual support and to Barley, Sorrel and Findlay who give me the space to work. A big thank you also to Barbara Smith, Joyce Mallinson, Claire Metson and Margaret Tomlinson for their many hours of stitching while working to tight deadlines.

The author and publishers would also like to thank the following companies for supplying materials for the projects or props for the photography.

david wood ART, Osgathorpe, Leicestershire for the frames; Bear Brothers, Chilton Foliat, Berkshire for the striped apron; Knot Just Wood, Wooten Wawen, Solihull for the egg cabinet; Craft Creations Ltd, Tottenham, London for the greetings card blanks; Scumble Goosie, Stroud, Gloucestershire for the heart tray; Blankers!, Honiton, Devon for the pencil pot and salt box; American Country Collection, Weybridge, Surrey for the American flags; Coats Craft UK, Darlington for evenweave linen, canvas and embroidery threads; DMC Creative World, Leicestershire for evenweave linen, linen bands and embroidery threads; Appleton Wools, Chiswick, London for the tapestry wools; the Inglestone Collection, Fairford, Gloucestershire for the stitching paper; Offray, Ashford, Middlesex for the gingham ribbons; Pinebrush Products, Coton Clanford, Stafford for the Colourman paints; Shaker, London for the peg board.

A WARD LOCK BOOK

First published in the UK 1997 by Ward Lock
Wellington House, 125 Strand, London WC2R OBB

A Cassell Imprint

Copyright ©1997 Dorothy Wood

Design by Richard Carr
Edited by Wendy Hobson
Illustrations by Nicola Gregory
Photography by Paul Bricknell

Distributed in the United States by Sterling Publishing Co., Inc.
387 Park Avenue South, New York, NY 1001–8810

A British Liibrary Cataloguing-in-Publication Data block for this book
may be obtained from the British Library

ISBN 0-7063-7626-9

Printed and bound by South China Printing Co. Ltd., Hong Kong

CONTENTS

INTRODUCTION

*I*NSPIRED by American crafts, such as stencilled furniture, patchwork quilts, Shaker boxes and hooked rugs, *American Country Cross Stitch* contains a wealth of beautiful designs which have been divided into four sections, each with its own distinct style: Pennsylvanian and Amish; Shaker, New England; contemporary. From brightly coloured Pennsylvanian motifs and appliqué quilts to the charming, whimsical designs on hooked rugs, the projects have been designed in the delightful and enormously popular country style and show the wide variety of ways in which cross stitch can be used. The charted designs are simple in form but have the innate sense of good design common to all American folk art so that the items you create from them will take pride of place in your home for many years to come.

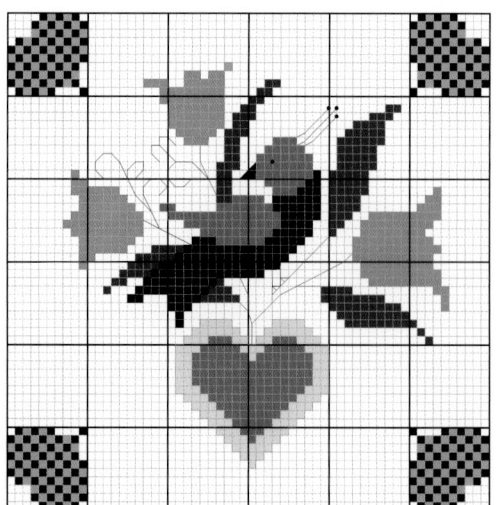

Birds, hearts and flowers are popular in folk art around the world. Here they have been combined to create two distinctly American designs. The Shaker Dove of Peace (above left) is surrounded by a pretty heart-shaped wreath. This delightful panel (above) is adapted from a classic Baltimore appliqué quilt.

A HISTORY OF AMERICAN COUNTRY STYLE

American country style began over two hundred years ago as new settlers strived to create comfortable homes for their families. Struggling with few tools and limited materials, the settlers made sturdy wooden furniture, with bed covers and rugs for warmth and comfort. Initially the furnishings were basic and simple, but in time people began to feel sufficiently well established to begin

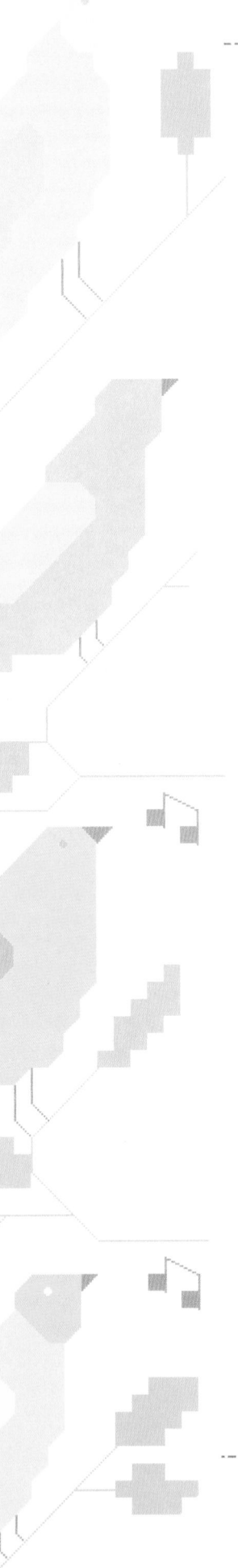

decorating these items. With no books for reference and only distant memories, the designs and motifs lost some of their original detail, but this was compensated for by an innate sense of good taste. Ordinary 'folk' with no formal training developed a simple, unpretentious approach and the creative traditions which were originally English or European became distinctly American. Although folk art was an integral part of all the rural settlements, the communities carried on their lives in isolation, therefore several different regional styles evolved. Amish and Shaker communities, set apart by their language or religion, developed unique styles while the Pennsylvanian Dutch and New England settlers carried on the strong craft traditions that they had brought with them from Europe and England.

The charming, naïve painted furniture and punched or painted tinware of the Pennsylvanian Dutch is what most people today would think of as folk art. Originally from Holland, Germany and Switzerland, the settlers began to recreate the art and craft of their homelands. Instead of carving their furniture, they painted it with bright colours using simple motifs such as tulips, birds, hearts and stars. These traditional designs, drawn from memory, were simpler than the original European folk art, and as the years went on the craftsmen added new motifs, such as the pomegranate and pineapple, and created some more unusual compositions. These distinctive designs have become very popular and are often stencilled rather than painted free-hand. Ever enthusiastic, but with little expertise, the Pennsylvanian Dutch also wrote and decorated simple manuscripts. These birth and baptism certificates are collectively known as Fracturs. Originally 'fraktur' was a typeface used for letters and documents but it came to mean any text or painting created around the same time. Fracturs contain delightful motifs, some drawn by skilled artists and others that have a delightful child-like quality that adapt very easily and successfully into cross stitch designs.

In contrast, the Shaker style has remained surprisingly plain. Shaker craftsmen aimed to make objects which were faultless. The now familiar chairs, oval boxes and furniture were developed purely from a pursuit of excellence. Following the guidance of their founder, Mother Ann Lee, the Shakers worked 'as if they had a thousand years to live, and as if they were to die tomorrow'. Successive generations refined the designs until they became the beautifully proportioned pieces we know today.

The Shakers had an unusual lifestyle. Living in a structured community, in family groups of up to a hundred members, they filled their days with worship and work. Shaker industries and farms prospered and they began to sell their surplus produce and homespun fabrics to the outside world. The Shakers also developed items such as decorative herbal gifts, cosmetics and lined boxes which they would never use themselves but which provide much of the inspiration for Shaker style today.

Although the Shakers thought they would live in the community for the whole of their lives, the American Civil War and industrialization intervened. Due mainly to their celibate lifestyle, numbers began to dwindle after 1860, because although they were grouped together and lived as families, they were not, in fact, related. The remaining Shakers looked to their late founder, Mother Ann Lee, for strength and inspiration. They produced brightly coloured manuscripts featuring delightful motifs such as the Tree of Life, the Dove of Peace and the Flower of Humility. These inspirational drawings present a dramatic contrast to the simple, austere Shaker home, and although never displayed were lovingly cared for by their owners, and now provide a rich source of design material for the cross stitcher.

The Harp of Joy and Dove of Peace (above) are just two of the simple motifs adapted for cross stitch from the Shaker Inspirational Drawings. The charming, colourful birds (opposite) were inspired by an original pen and ink fractur bookmark showing thirty-six birds in a tree.

Patchwork and appliqué quilts were made in abundance by the early settlers and provide perhaps the greatest store of inspiration. The standard of workmanship varied considerably because girls began to make quilt tops at an early age and by the time they were engaged were expected to have thirteen quilts ready. The quilts were generally assembled just before they married and so the final thirteenth bridal quilt was usually the best of all. Different communities developed their own styles. The New Englanders developed the patchwork block and made ornate appliqué patterns, whereas Amish quilts had one overall geometric design

Amish quilts are unique because they reflect their simple lifestyle. The Amish have not changed the way they live since the eighteenth century and the dark, unpatterned fabrics they use in clothes and furnishing reflects their belief that God created everyone equal and that no one person should stand out from the group. With only a few basic patterns, such as the diamond and bar designs, the Amish use strong colour contrast to great effect and produce beautifully balanced designs.

New Englanders, on the other hand, collected scraps of fabric from old clothes and bed linen and pieced together quilts using patchwork or appliqué. The patchwork quilts were usually abstract in design and new patterns were created to celebrate important events. Patchwork blocks such as the Star of North Carolina and the Virginia Star were created after the New England territories became States. The pictorial Baltimore quilts possibly evolved from the ornate tapestries and embroidered bed covers popular in seventeenth-century Europe. Bold plant forms, exotic birds and tropical fruits printed on early fabrics imported by the East India Company were very popular, but because these fabrics were in short supply, the resourceful New Englanders adapted the designs for appliqué and used their imagination to create some fabulous quilts. As wallpaper and printed fabrics were scarce, stencilling, which has seen a recent renaissance, was used by the early settlers to decorate their homes. Bed covers, walls, floors and furniture

Stars have been popular in American folk art since colonial times. This eight-pointed star was inspired by traditional patchwork quilts.

The patriotic five-pointed star has been a recurring motif since the first star-spangled banner flew in 1812.

were covered in complex designs inspired by seventeenth-century Elizabethan tapestries. These simplified forms and creative patterns translate easily into cross stitch and can be used to decorate bed linen, soft furnishings and other items in the home.

Patterns, designs and methods of decoration, which were created out of necessity and a desire to make homes as comfortable and welcoming as possible, have again become popular in their own right. Natural linens and homespun gingham are much in evidence, as are hand-made rugs and painted furniture. Contemporary Americans are once again using traditional skills to create beautiful designs for their homes. This sense of history is reflected in the current trend toward patriotism and the use of the American flag in contemporary designs. In many ways, American folk art has come full circle and the cross stitch designs in this book reflect the pride all Americans have in their country.

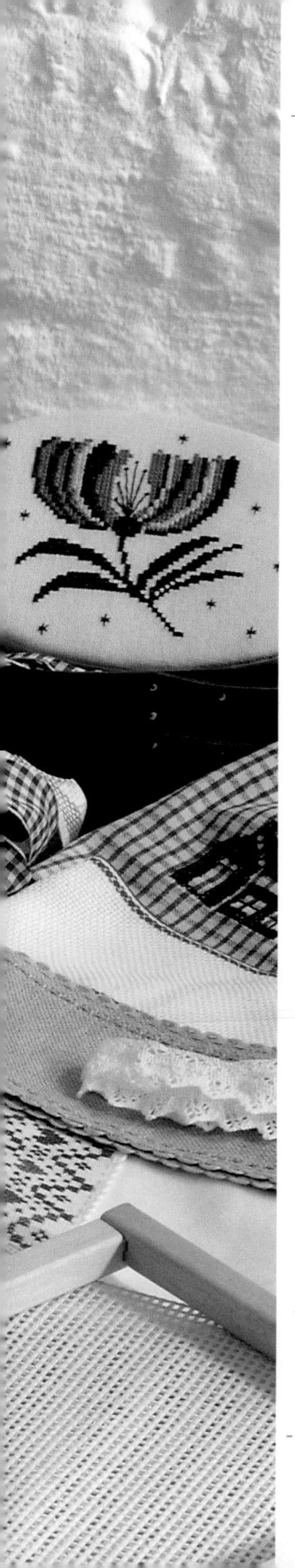

MATERIALS AND TECHNIQUES

THERE are over forty country-style projects in this book and the level of cross stitching skill required from project to project varies considerably. Simple projects like the pillowcase border (page 84) and the herb heart hanging (page 106) are ideal for beginners, while more complex designs such as the fractur picture (page 42) and the watermelon picture (page 122) can be tackled by those with a little more skill and experience. All the projects have detailed lists of the materials required and clear instructions about stitching and making up. There is a technique section showing the basic sewing skills needed to complete the designs and some of the projects have clear diagrams to illustrate more complicated making-up steps. Whatever your stitching and sewing expertise there is a wide selection of designs to choose from – something for everyone with a love for country style.

FABRICS

Most cross stitch is worked following a pre-planned design which has been drawn out on graph paper. As a result it is recommended and probably essential to stitch the design on a purpose-made even-weave fabric. These are specially woven fabrics which have an even number of warp (vertical) threads to weft (horizontal). The number of threads in each 1in (2.5cm) is known as the count. Finer fabrics have a higher count, that is more threads to the inch or centimetre.

1 Linen
2 Canvas
3 Aida
4 Linen band
5 Evenweave

Evenweaves

There are two main types of evenweave fabric: those woven into blocks with clearly defined holes and those made with a simple plain weave.

Binca, Aida, Ainring and Hardanger all belong to the first group. The count of these fabrics indicates the number of stitches to 1in (2.5cm). Aida is probably the most widely used fabric. It is easy to stitch with clearly defined holes and comes in a wide range of counts and colours. Nevertheless the majority of projects in this book use fabric from the second group. Originally only available in pure linen, there is now a wide range of evenweave fabrics with different handling properties, including pure cotton, cotton and viscose, or linen and cotton mix. Although slightly more difficult to work, these purpose-made fabrics give a very professional finish to cross stitch designs and are worth the extra effort. The count of the linen-type fabrics indicates the number of threads to 1in (2.5cm). Stitches are usually worked over two threads, therefore a 28-count linen is equivalent to a 14-count Aida. The two fabrics are interchangeable and any of the projects can be worked on Aida if preferred.

Canvas

A few of the projects in this book have been stitched in tapestry wool on canvas. This is a methodical type of cross stitch worked on a much larger scale so that even large cushions are completed in a surprisingly short time.

There are three types of canvas: single, double and interlocking. Single canvas is evenly woven with single warp (vertical) threads going over and under single weft (horizontal) threads. Double thread canvas is woven with pairs of threads, and stitches are normally worked over two threads. Interlock canvas looks similar to single canvas but the warp threads are twisted between each weft thread to prevent the weave being distorted. Since all these canvasses produce a similar result, the one you use really comes down to personal preference, but do buy the best quality you can afford.

Cross stitch requires a larger mesh size than needlepoint. Tapestry wool covers a large mesh 7-count canvas with an attractive chunky look. If you tend to stitch quite tightly you may find an 8-count canvas gives better coverage but the finished design will be slightly smaller.

Waste Canvas

Waste canvas is a single canvas which is used as a temporary grid for stitching on to ready-made items, such as aprons and tea towels and on to non-evenweave fabrics.

A piece of canvas at least 1in (2.5cm) larger than the design is tacked over the area to be stitched and the cross stitch worked through the grid. Stitch in a stabbing motion, taking the needle up and down in the centre of the mesh. Extra care must be taken to ensure the stitches are even and not pulled too tightly. Once the cross stitch is complete, the canvas has to removed. Either fray the first 1in (2.5cm) of canvas and then pull the threads out one at a time using a pair of tweezers if required, or wet the canvas slightly by wrapping in a damp towel, then pull them out by hand. This loosens the weave but can leave a sticky residue.

Stitching Paper

Stitching paper is just that, paper with a regular grid of holes for stitching cross stitch. It is a non-fray material and a perfect base for small cross stitch designs which completely cover the background. It is ideal for greetings cards and for cross stitch decorations or small panels which need to be trimmed close to the design. Care must be taken when stitching through paper as it can tear easily. Make sure you are using the correct size of needle and work in a stabbing motion, taking the thread up and down through the holes in the paper. The paper can be repaired with sticky tape and the holes repunched with a large needle if required.

Preparing Evenweave Fabric

The size of fabric specified in each project allows plenty of room for the cross stitch design plus extra for neatening the edge to prevent fraying. Small or quickly stitched projects may be worked without neatening the edge, but for larger projects, especially those worked on linen, it is worth taking the extra time required. Linen can fray considerably and you may find yourself short of fabric when it comes to making up the design. Overlocking or zigzag stitch is the quickest method, recommended when the design is going to be made into a picture, bag or cushion. Alternatively turn under a small hem and hem stitch or oversew to secure the edge.

1. Stitching paper
2. 10-count waste canvas
3. 14-count waste canvas

$\mathcal{T}$HREADS AND $\mathcal{E}$QUIPMENT

There are many different types of embroidery thread suitable for cross stitch. Although stranded cotton is seen as the standard yarn, other threads such as flower thread, coton perlé, coton à broder, tapestry wool, crewel wool and even some metallic threads can be used with equal success. There are three different threads used in this book, each keeping the feel and look of traditional American country style.

Stranded Cotton

Stranded cotton is the most popular cross stitch embroidery thread, renowned for its versatility and uniformity. Available in over four hundred different shades, it can be separated into six strands, making it suitable for stitching on a wide range of fabrics. As a rough guide, use one strand on 18–20-count evenweave, two on 14–16-count evenweave and three strands on 10–12-count evenweave. Two or three colours of stranded cotton can be worked together in the needle to achieve different effects.

Flower Thread

Flower thread is a single thickness cotton thread which has an attractive, rustic look. It is particularly suitable for working on 28-count linen and is equivalent to approximately two strands of stranded cotton. The thread is not as uniform as stranded cotton but suits country-style designs. The colour range is less extensive but new colours are being added to the range all the time as its popularity grows. Flower thread can become 'fluffy' when stitching through linen or non-evenweave fabric. Tailor's wax, which is available from haberdashers, can be used to prevent this. Pull each length of thread over the edge of the wax block before stitching in the usual way.

Tapestry Wool

Although generally associated with needlepoint, tapestry wool is also suitable for cross stitch. Worked on a chunky 7-count canvas, it makes a wonderful hardwearing covers for cushions and stools. When buying yarn for tapestry wool projects remember that the quantities given are only approximate. Amounts used during stitching vary from person to person depending on how loosely or tightly they work. If possible buy all you need at the same time as dye batches differ slightly and even a subtle change would be noticeable, especially in background areas.

Blending Colours

Wonderful effects can be achieved by 'blending' or mixing threads in the needle. Sometimes this technique is used to shade from one colour to the next using two similar threads in the needle, but it can also add texture by using two different colours to produce a mottled effect. Try experimenting by stitching a colour wheel using only primary and secondary colours. The tertiary colours – such as blue-green, yellow-orange and so on – can be created by blending the two adjacent colours together.

Needles

Tapestry needles have blunt ends which pass through evenweave fabrics without splitting or fraying them. They come in a range of sizes from 13 to 28. The correct size for each project is given in the instructions, but as a general rule the needle should

take the thread comfortably and be able to pass through the weave of the fabric without pulling or distorting it.

Frames

It is very much a personal choice whether or not to use an embroidery frame. Most purpose-made evenweave fabrics have a fairly stiff finish and can be worked without a frame. If necessary, press the fabric on the reverse side with a steam iron from time to time to restore the finish as you work.

Embroidery frames and hoops come in various forms and sizes. They can help to make stitches and tension even throughout a piece of work. Choose a size and type that is comfortable for you. Linen-type evenweaves can be fitted into a small hoop which fits easily in the hand and is moved as work progresses. Cover the inner hoop with a layer of white tape to protect the fabric and always remember to take your work out of the hoop when you have finished for the day.

Aida and canvas can be distorted in a small hoop and should be stretched on a larger frame. Rotary frames are ideal as the canvas is stitched on to a fabric strip and rolled on to bars to keep the weave straight. Small square or rectangular projects can be stretched over interlocking bar frames. The side bars for these frames are available in pairs of different sizes which are interchangeable.

Scissors

You will need a small pair of embroidery scissors for snipping threads on the reverse of the cross stitch and a larger pair of dressmaking scissors to cut fabric. Avoid using sewing scissors to cut paper as they will quickly become blunt.

Basic Stitches

Cross Stitch

Different people work cross stitch in different ways. Being left-handed, I tend to work from the top of the design, working rows of half stitches down, then completing the cross stitch on the way back up. Right-handed people usually work across the design from left to right. Regardless of which way you work, the top stitch should always face in the same direction otherwise the finished cross stitch looks untidy. Sometimes it can be helpful to put a pin in the work indicating the direction of the top stitch. This can be particularly useful when working a square border where the linen may be turned to repeat the design.

Cross stitch can either be worked as an individual stitch or as a row of half stitches which are completed on the way back. The second method is generally quicker and gives more even results over larger areas.

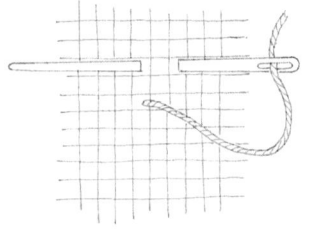
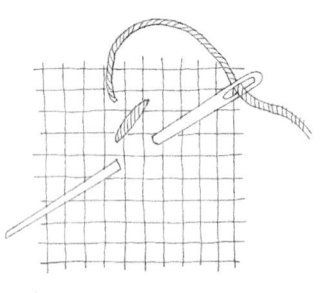

The single cross stitch method produces a slightly raised stitch. Each stitch is completed before moving on to the next and is ideal for working small details and odd stitches in the design.

To cover large areas, complete the cross stitch in two journeys. Stitch a row of half stitches, then complete the cross on the way back. Whether you work across the linen or down and up, the needle goes through the fabric in the same direction on each journey allowing a rhythm to be achieved and neat, even stitches to be produced.

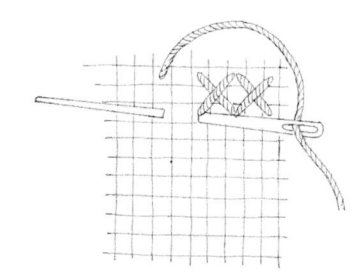 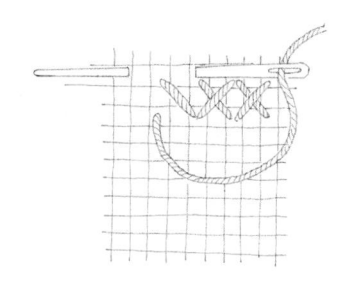

To stitch a row from right to left, work single cross stitches and take the thread across the back of the fabric ready to start the next stitch. This produces a slightly raised line of stitches which could be used in a border or as an outline.

Half Cross Stitch

Some of the charts in this book contain half blocks to provide more detailed shaping in the design. These blocks can either be worked as a simple half stitches or with the three-quarter version. The latter gives a more solid effect and can produce a distinct line round the edge of a design.

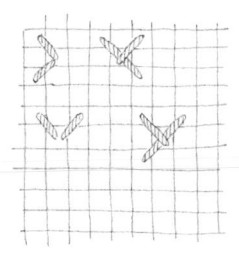

A half cross stitch is worked diagonally over one thread of linen, or into the centre of a block of stitches if working on Aida.

If working the three-quarter stitch, sew the long diagonal first and then catch the stitch down with the short diagonal.

Back Stitch

This is a solid, slightly raised stitch used to outline areas of cross stitch and work design lines on top of cross stitch, such as the veins in

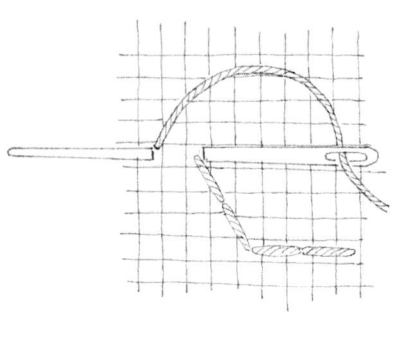

a leaf. When working diagonally, try to keep the stitches an even size and avoid using long stitches. If the cross stitch is worked with two strands of cotton, the back stitch is usually worked with a single strand.

Work back stitch from right to left, making stitches the same size as the cross stitch where possible. When stitching diagonally, it may be necessary to sew into the middle of a block of Aida or over one thread of linen to keep the stitch length even.

Marking Cross Stitch

This is a reversible variation of cross stitch which is ideal for stitching lettering or monograms on household linen or reversible items. Use a single strand of cotton to begin as most of the stitches are recrossed while working this method.

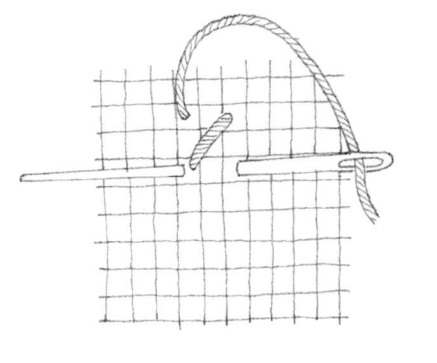 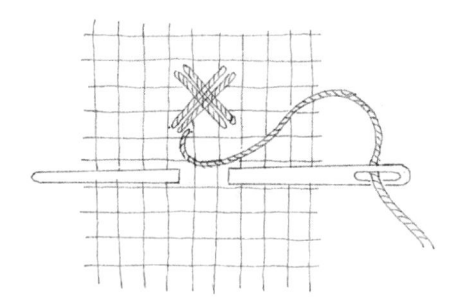

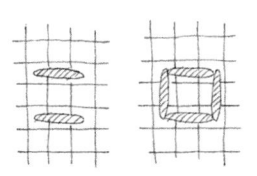

Follow the diagrams carefully and note which stitches have to be recrossed to make complete squares on the reverse side. The diagram (left) shows what the stitch looks like on the reverse side at each stage.

French Knot

French knots are small, raised stitches used to add texture to a piece, and can introduce spots of colour over large expanses of cross stitch. The stitch can also be used for small details such as eyes, flower centres and tiny berries.

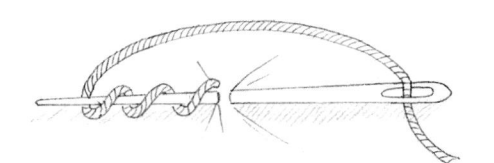

Bring the needle and thread through the fabric where the French knot is to be worked. Take a tiny stitch close to where the thread emerges and wrap this thread round the needle three times. Use your thumb to hold the wrapped threads as you pull the needle through to form the knot. Insert the needle close to the knot and take the thread back through to the reverse side. If you want to change the size of the French knot, increase or decrease the thickness of the embroidery thread rather than the number of twists round the needle.

Slip Stitch

Slip stitch is one of the most useful stitches for finishing fabric projects. Ideal for closing gaps in cushions, attaching cross stitch panels to other fabric and stitching small hems, it should be invisible when completed.

Take a small stitch under a couple of threads of fabric and slip the needle through the hem for ¼in (5mm). Bring the needle out and take a second tiny stitch in the fabric. Continue to slip stitch in this way to the end. The tiny stitch is always through the front fabric and the longer stitch through the back fabric.

STITCHING TECHNIQUES

Working from a Chart

Counted cross stitch is one of the simplest forms of embroidery. Each stitch is represented by a colour block or symbol on a grid. Work one cross stitch for each block. Half blocks can be stitched as half or three-quarter stitches. The different colour blocks and symbols are given in a key which lists the make and colour of thread to be used. The project instructions explain where to begin,

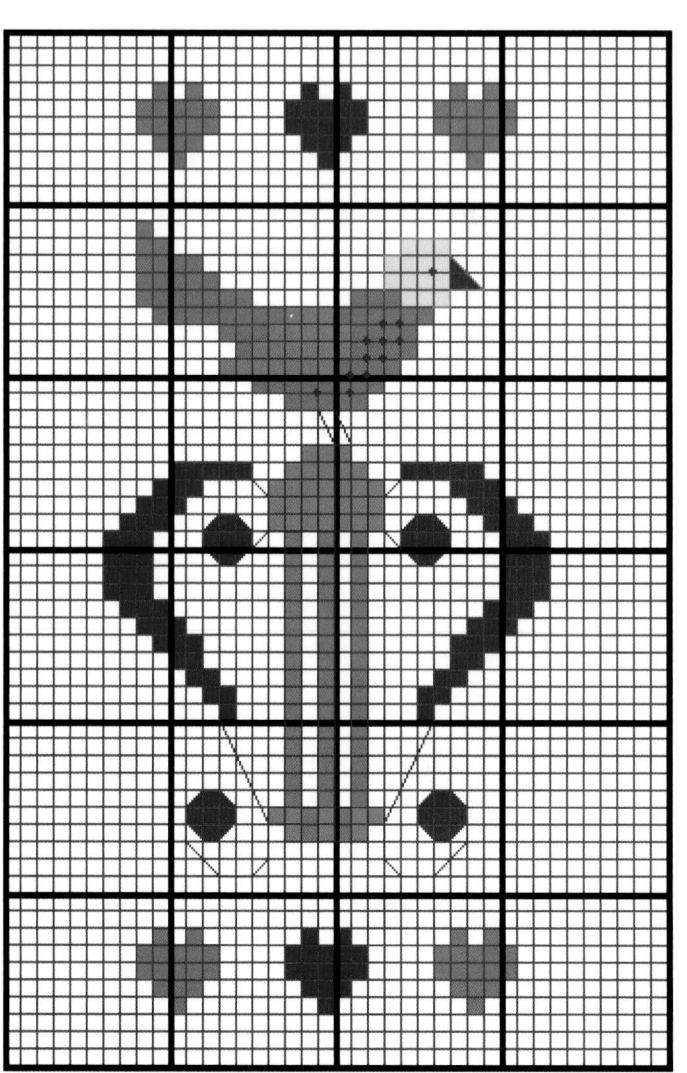

STITCH KEY
▓ Single cross stitch
◣ Half cross stitch
═ Backstitch
⁙ French knot

the number of strands of cotton to use and how many threads to stitch over. Back stitch is shown as a solid line indicating the colour and position of the stitch. French knots are shown as a dot.

Altering the Design

Cross stitch charts are adaptable and can be altered to create designs suitable for use on different projects. The size and colours in the design can be changed if required. Perhaps you want to alter a design to match a particular colour scheme in your house or so that you can use a different colour of linen. Select the colours you would like to use and change the thread numbers on the key. Aim for a similar depth of colour for each alternative thread and stitch a small sample of the design to check that your choice of threads work together before beginning.

The same cross stitch chart can be used to stitch designs in several different sizes. You could use the same motif to make matching cushions and tie-backs by stitching one on linen and the other on canvas. The size of the cross stitch design is determined by the count of the fabric or, in the case of linen, by the number of threads each stitch is worked over. The design size can be altered by increasing or decreasing the count or the number of threads you stitch over. As a rough guide, a design which is 84 stitches square will measure 6in (15cm) on 14-count fabric, only 4¾in (12cm) on 18-count fabric and increase to 8¼in (21cm) on 10-count fabric.

Working a Repeat

Sometimes, because of restrictions in space, only part of a chart is shown. Shelf or curtain borders, for example, often have a single motif or block design which is repeated. The project instructions explain exactly where to stitch the next motif. If it is a repeat, begin in the centre of the border and continue the design on either side as far as required.

Working from an Alphabet Chart

Many different initials, names, monograms and mottoes can be stitched from the letters in an alphabet chart and it would be impossible to chart all the possibilities for each project. The letters you need can be copied on to graph paper and the spacing sorted out before you start to stitch. Although it appears that letters are evenly spaced, they often have a different number of threads between each letter to accommodate the shape. Wide letters such as A, M and W usually look better if stitched closer to the adjacent letter. Look closely at the letters in this chart and note that there is no real space between the M and W. Nevertheless the letters, dots and hearts all look evenly spaced. If there had been equal spaces between the letters the design would look stretched out and uneven.

Decide which letters you are going to use and draw the first one out on graph paper. Leave one row of squares between straight-sided letters and position the wider letters so that the space looks the same. If required, dots or tiny motifs can be added between the letters in the same way so that the overall effect is of evenly spaced letters.

Monograms

Monograms are groups of two or more letters intertwined or over-lapping to make an attractive motif. These can be worked out quite easily using tracing paper and graph paper.

1 Select two letters and draw them individually on graph paper with a coloured pen. Trace over one of the letters, turn the tracing paper over and go over the lines again in soft pencil on the reverse side.

2 Position the tracing paper the right way up over the other letter so that they overlap. Move the tracing paper until you have a satisfactory arrangement and draw over the letter to transfer on to the graph paper.

3 Colour the transferred letter with a different coloured pen, making the letters appear to interlink by over and underlapping parts of the letters. Draw the monogram out again on fresh graph paper ready to begin the cross stitching.

Beginning the Cross Stitch

Every project has detailed instructions explaining which count of fabric to use, how to mark the exact position of the cross stitch and where it is best to begin, which is generally in the centre. Usually the centre point of the design can be found by folding the fabric in half lengthways and then in half crossways. The resulting creases can be sufficient to begin, but larger pieces and pictures need to have more permanent guidelines tacked along the centre folds. The tacked lines help when counting threads on larger pieces of linen and are invaluable markers when stretching the finished work.

Begin cross stitch by bringing the needle up through the fabric and leaving a short tail on the reverse side. Either hold the tail and catch it under the next few stitches or sew it under the threads later. Finish a row of cross stitch by sewing the end in under the thread on the reverse side and trimming the end.

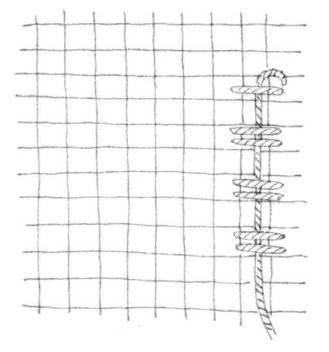

Care of the Fabric

Always wash your hands before stitching. Take the cross stitch out of the hoop at the end of the day and keep your work in a clean pillowslip when not stitching. Sometimes, despite following these common-sense guidelines, the fabric can still look rather grubby by the time the project is finished. Luckily all evenweave fabrics can be successfully laundered and all the threads used in this book are colourfast. If necessary, wash the cross stitch gently in warm water using a detergent suitable for delicate fabrics. Rinse thoroughly, roll the fabric up in a towel to remove the excess water, then leave it to dry flat. While it is still slightly damp, press the cross stitch on the reverse side. If the fabric is completely dry use a damp cloth or steam iron to remove the creases.

Stretching Canvas

Projects worked in wool on canvas need to be stretched or 'blocked' while damp to even out the stitches and remove any creases. Don't cut away any excess canvas until this has been completed.

Stretching or 'blocking' is done on a block of wood. This has to be larger than the project and soft enough to take large map pins, drawing pins or, if necessary, carpet tacks.

Lay the canvas on top of the block of wood and spray lightly with water without soaking the cross stitch. Insert a map pin at the centre top of the canvas, pull the cross stitch down slightly and insert another map pin at the centre bottom. Keeping the canvas straight, work out from the centre top, pulling the canvas slightly and inserting map pins every 1in (2.5cm). Stretch the sides, then the bottom and use a large set square to check that the corners are square. Leave the cross stitch to dry completely, away from direct heat. When it is completely dry, which can take several days, remove the pins and trim the canvas to leave a ⅝in (1.5cm) seam allowance.

Making-up Techniques

All the cross stitch designs in this book have been made into items such as pictures, cushions, bags, table linen and book covers. There are attractive projects for the home as well as some which would make welcome gifts. Whatever the project, it is essential that as much care is taken in making up as in the stitching of the cross stitch. Many of the projects require basic dressmaking skills but are easy to make following the detailed instructions. Some of the more common techniques are outlined here.

Trimming Seam Allowances

One of the easiest ways to achieve a professional finish is by trimming seams carefully. Reducing excess bulk on the inside allows the fabric to lie flat and prevents unsightly bumps on the right side.

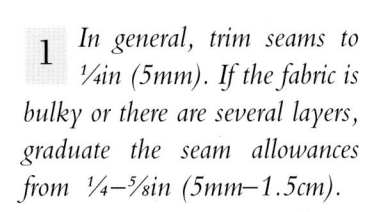 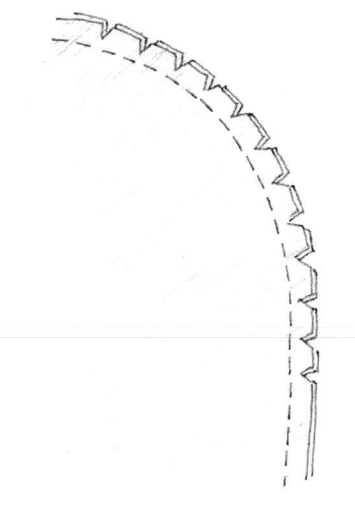 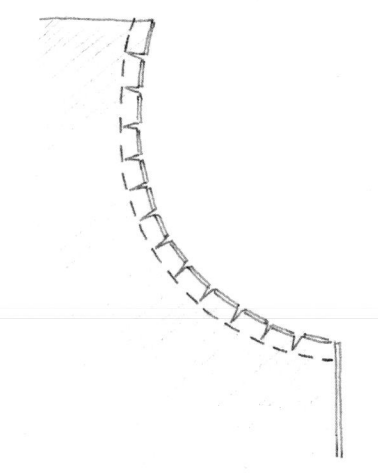

1 *In general, trim seams to ¼in (5mm). If the fabric is bulky or there are several layers, graduate the seam allowances from ¼–⅝in (5mm–1.5cm).*

2 *Snip inward-facing curves and notch outward facing curves. Trim diagonally across corners close to the stitching.*

3 *Wherever possible, press seams open before turning through. When making cushions or similar projects, ease out corners carefully until they are square and roll seams between finger and thumb before pressing.*

Mitred Corners

Mitring corners reduces bulk and produces a neat, professional finish on table linen.

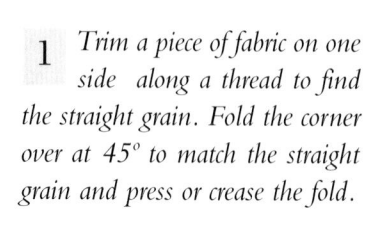

1 *Trim the evenweave exactly along the straight grain by cutting straight along a thread. Fold the hem and carefully press in position. (Exact measurements are given in the instructions.) Open out the hem and fold the corner over so that the diagonal fold falls exactly across the hemline crease. Press the diagonal fold line then open out and trim to ¼in (5mm).*

2 *Fold the hem again along the pressed lines to form a neat mitred corner. Tack and stitch the hem in position, then slip stitch the edges of the mitred corner.*

Bias Binding

Bias binding can be bought ready made or made from strips of matching or contrasting fabric. Both types can be used to bind edges, make piping or be made into rouleaux. Home-made binding can be made any width or length required.

1 *Trim a piece of fabric on one side along a thread to find the straight grain. Fold the corner over at 45° to match the straight grain and press or crease the fold.*

2 *Open out the fold and mark parallel lines the required width using tailor's chalk and a ruler. (Exact measurements are given in the instructions.) Cut along the lines.*

3 *To join the strips, lay one over the other as shown with right sides facing. Pin and stitch where the edges cross over. Press the seam open and trim off the little triangles to align the fabric.*

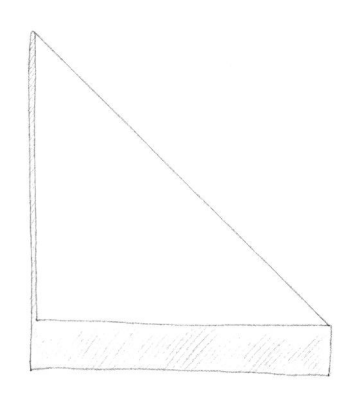

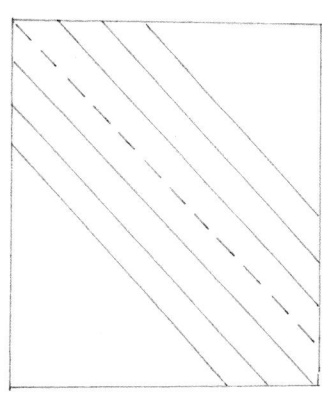

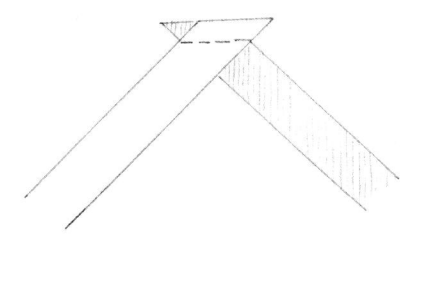

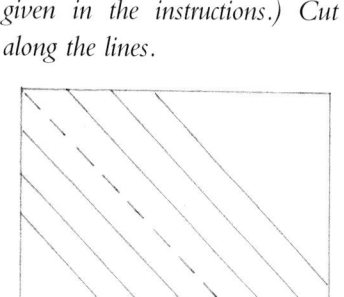

Attaching Bias Binding

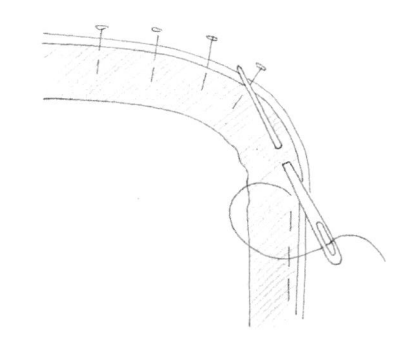

1 Cut a bias strip four times the finished width required and join sufficient
lengths together to fit round the edge of the project. Carefully trim the seam
allowance on the project to the finished width. Pin and tack the bias strip along
the seam allowance with the raw edges together and right sides facing. Stretch or
ease the bias strip to fit flat round corners. Overlap the ends, turning under the
end of the underneath bias strip.

2 Stitch along the seam line and press flat. Fold the other raw edge
into the centre of the bias strip and fold over again so that it touches
the stitching. Pin, tack and hem just inside the machine stitching.

Piping

1 Measure round the edge of the project and make a 1½in (4cm) bias strip
about 2in (5cm) longer than required. Cut a piece of piping cord the same
length. Fold the bias strip in half along its length and tuck the cord inside. Tack
close to the cord to secure.

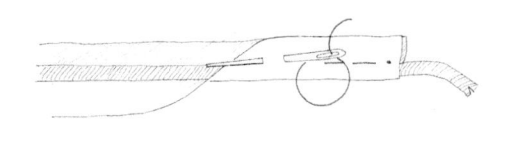

2 Beginning in the middle of one side, pin the piping round the edge of the
project with the right sides facing. Match the raw edges together and snip
into the seam allowance at the corners.

3 Overlap the ends of the piping and mark where they cross with pins.
Open out the last few inches and join the bias strips together as shown
below. Trim the piping cord to fit and tack in place. Machine stitch close to the
cord using a zipper foot attachment. Follow the project instructions to finish.

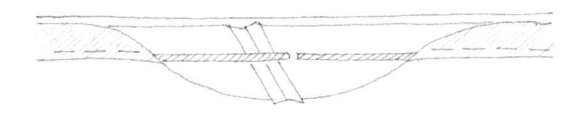

Stretching

Projects such as pictures, books and greetings cards have to be stretched before being made up. Although it is preferable to stretch embroideries using thread so that they can be removed from the backing or frame and cleaned in the future, small projects, which may be kept for a limited time, can be quickly stretched using double-sided tape.

STRETCHING USING TAPE

Cut the card the required size and stick double-sided tape all round the edges quite close to the edge. Lay the embroidery face down and position the card carefully on top with the tape facing up. Trim the seam allowance to ⅝in (1.5cm), remove the backing paper from the tape, and stretch the fabric over the edge of the board and on to the tape in the middle of each side. Mitre the corners carefully (see page 30) and stick down firmly all the way round. For extra neat corners the mitred edges can be slip stitched together.

STRETCHING USING THREAD

Dust, moisture and acid can cause the fabric and threads to deteriorate over time, therefore cross stitch designs which are to be hung and hopefully kept for years must be stretched and mounted with care. This can be left to the professionals if you prefer, but it can be done at home following a few simple rules. Practise the technique on a small piece first.

Use an acid-free mountboard if possible or back the cross stitch with a piece of fine white cotton before stretching. Fit plastic spacers round the edge of the frame between the glass and the linen to protect the surface from condensation, and seal the back of the frame with tape to keep out the dust.

1 Measure the mountboard and mark the centre point on each side. Lay the embroidery face down on a flat surface and position the mountboard on top, matching the centre marks to the tacked guidelines.

2 Fold the top edge of the linen over the side of the board. Insert a pin at the centre point through the linen into the edge of the mountboard. Repeat on the other three sides. With the straight grain of the linen running along the edge of the board, insert pins every 1in (2.5cm) on all sides.

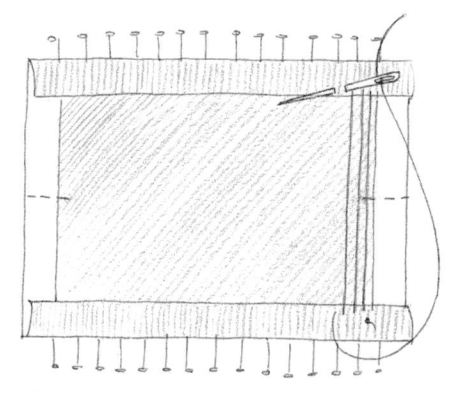

3 Thread the needle with a long length of strong thread. Sew two sides of the linen together across the back. Add extra lengths of thread as you go, joining them in with an overhand knot.

Overhand knot

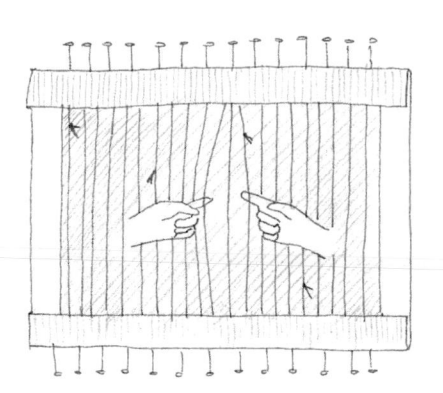

4 Before sewing in the end, pull up each long thread in turn with your fingers to take out the slack. The overhand knots will feed through the linen as you go. Fold over the other two sides and stitch together in the same way. Remove the pins once the stretching is complete.

5 Insert the stretched cross stitch into the frame of your choice and seal the edges with a strong brown tape.

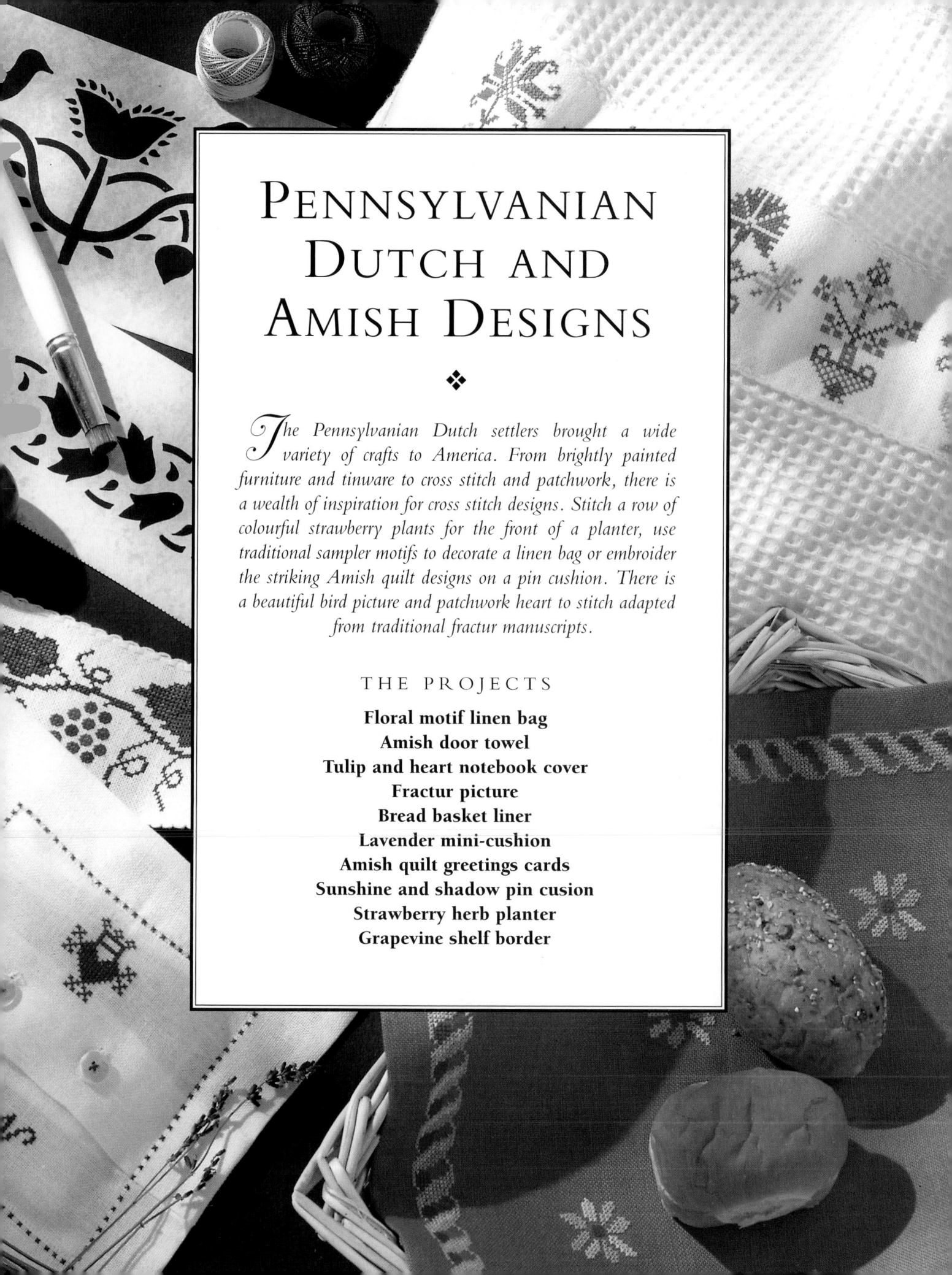

PENNSYLVANIAN DUTCH AND AMISH DESIGNS

❖

The Pennsylvanian Dutch settlers brought a wide variety of crafts to America. From brightly painted furniture and tinware to cross stitch and patchwork, there is a wealth of inspiration for cross stitch designs. Stitch a row of colourful strawberry plants for the front of a planter, use traditional sampler motifs to decorate a linen bag or embroider the striking Amish quilt designs on a pin cushion. There is a beautiful bird picture and patchwork heart to stitch adapted from traditional fractur manuscripts.

THE PROJECTS

Floral motif linen bag
Amish door towel
Tulip and heart notebook cover
Fractur picture
Bread basket liner
Lavender mini-cushion
Amish quilt greetings cards
Sunshine and shadow pin cusion
Strawberry herb planter
Grapevine shelf border

FLORAL MOTIF LINEN BAG

*T*HIS *extremely spacious linen bag is quick and easy to make using two white waffle-weave cotton hand towels. The pretty green, tan and golden yellow flower pots are traditional Amish sampler motifs from the early nineteenth century.*

MATERIALS

❖ 20in (50cm) of 3in (7.5cm) wide scalloped-edge linen band, Zweigart E7312, 39 stitches
❖ Anchor Nordin flower thread 216, 365, 891
❖ size 24 tapestry needle
❖ tailor's wax (optional)
❖ two white waffle-weave hand towels, approx. 20 x 30in (50 x 76cm)
❖ tape measure
❖ scissors
❖ white sewing thread
❖ pins
❖ needle
❖ 1¼ yds (1.2m) size 6 piping cord
❖ large safety pin
❖ wide-toothed comb

TO STITCH

1 Turn under the ends of the linen band and machine stitch close to the edge. Fold the band in half lengthways to find the centre, then begin stitching the right-hand motif two threads down from the scalloped edge.

2 Work each motif over two threads with a single thickness of flower thread. You may find it easier to stitch flower thread through linen if each length is lightly waxed before use.

3 Work the two motifs on the left of the centre flower pot, then repeat on the other side with a mirror image, completing five motifs in all.

4 Press on the reverse side with a damp cloth.

TO MAKE UP

1 Cut 4in (10cm) from the length of both towels. Turn under the raw edges ¼in (5mm) and machine stitch. Measure 7in (18cm) up from this neatened edge on one of the towels and mark in the centre of the towel with a pin. Find the centre of the linen band and position above the pin on the right side of the towel. Pin along both long edges and stitch through the decorative scalloped edge.

2 Pin the towels together with right sides facing. Beginning and finishing 7in (18cm) from the top edge of the towels, machine down the sides and along the bottom edge. Press the seams open.

3 Flatten out one corner of the linen bag. Layer the side and bottom seams together and pin in position

Anchor Nordin flower thread

CROSS STITCH KEY
- ■ Anchor 216
- ■ Anchor 891
- ■ Anchor 365

along the open seam. Measure 3in (7.5cm) along the seam from the corner and mark a line with pins at right angles to the seam. Tack and stitch through all the layers along the marked line. Zigzag the seam close to the stitching and trim. Repeat on the other corner and turn through to the wrong side.

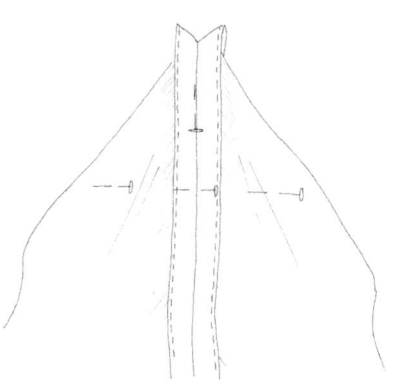

4 Fold over the top edge of the towels to the inside so that the fold is about 3in (7.5cm) from the stitched side seam. Pin, tack and stitch round the linen bag where the side seam ends and again 1¼in (3cm) closer to the folded edge to form a casing. Remove the tacking thread and press.

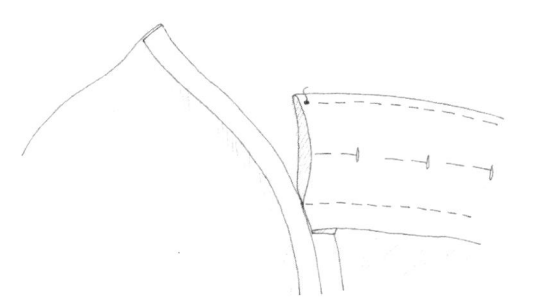

5 Cut the piping cord in half. Using the safety pin, thread one length through the casing on one side and back along the other side. Thread the second cord through from the other side of the bag in the opposite direction. Tie each pair of ends together in a simple overhand knot, leaving ends of about 3in (7.5cm).

6 Unravel the ends of the cord and comb the loose threads with a wide-toothed comb to make a tassel. Trim the end neatly and repeat with the other cord ends to complete. Pull the tassel ends and tie the cords in a loose bow to hang from a coat hook or door handle.

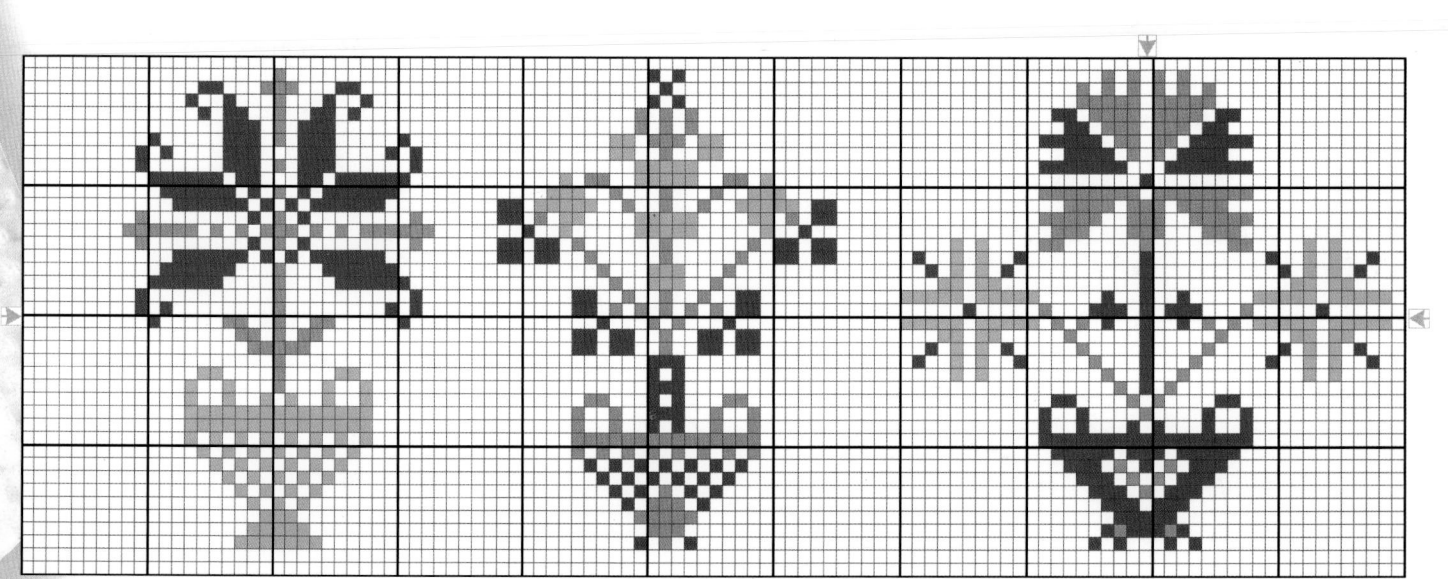

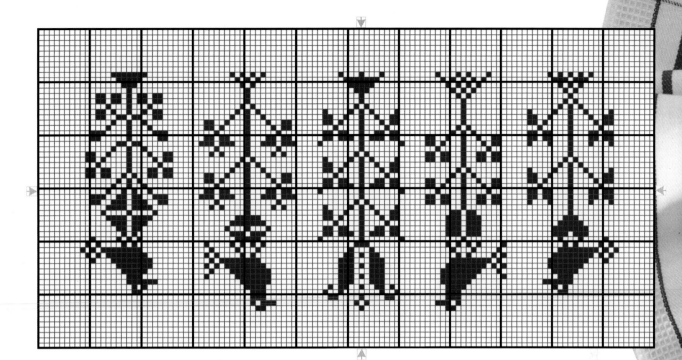

AMISH DOOR TOWEL

*T*RADITIONAL Amish door towels made from homespun linen
had an embroidered panel across the top and were hung by
loops on the back of the kitchen door. This way of hanging lets
the towel dry quickly and keeps it off the floor!

MATERIALS

- ❖ fine white waffle-weave hand towel 20 x 35in (50 x 89cm)
- ❖ Anchor Nordin flower thread 133
- ❖ size 24 tapestry needle
- ❖ tailor's wax (optional)
- ❖ scissors
- ❖ 14in (36cm) of ¼in (5mm) white tape
- ❖ pins
- ❖ white sewing thread

TO STITCH

1 The design has been worked directly on to the fabric using the waffle weave as a grid. Alternatively you could stitch on evenweave linen or gingham fabric and attach the panel to the top of the towel.

2 Count the number of squares across the towel and adjust the spacing between the motifs if required. Fold the towel in half lengthways to find the centre line.

3 Begin the centre motif eight squares down from the top border. Work the cross stitch using a single thickness of flower thread. Waxing each length of flower thread makes it easier to stitch through the towel. Stitch the remaining motifs evenly spaced on either side.

4 Press on the reverse side with a damp cloth.

CROSS STITCH KEY
Anchor Nordin flower thread
■ Anchor 133

TO MAKE UP

1 Cut the fringe from the top of the towel. Turn down and pin a narrow double hem along the top edge.

2 Cut the tape in half. Fold each piece in half and tuck the ends inside the narrow hem leaving a 2in (5cm) loop hanging out of each corner.

3 Machine stitch the narrow hem and stitch several times over the ends to secure the loops. Hang the towel from hooks on the back of the door or from a peg board.

TULIP AND HEART
NOTEBOOK COVER

*T*HIS *colourful and surprisingly contemporary looking tulip and heart motif was adapted from a lavishly decorated baptismal record, hand-drawn in 1868. As the traditional fractur style also included text, you could add some initials to the design.*

MATERIALS

❖ 12 x 16in (30 x 40cm) 28-count natural Quaker cloth, Zweigart 3993
❖ tacking thread
❖ needle
❖ tape measure
❖ pins
❖ Anchor stranded cotton 218, 306, 1028, 1036
❖ size 24 tapestry needle
❖ A5 size notebook
❖ double-sided tape
❖ scissors
❖ 8 x 12in (20 x 30cm) iron-on wadding
❖ bodkin or large needle

TO STITCH

1 Fold the linen in half crossways and tack a guideline down the fold. Measure 5½in (14cm) in from the right-hand side of the linen and mark with a pin. Measure 6½in (16.5cm) down from the top edge to mark the centre point of the design, which should be just above the middle of the cover of the book. Tack guidelines out from the centre.

2 Work the back stitch first using two strands of cotton. Once complete, work the cross stitch using two strands of cotton over two threads of linen. Finish the embroidery design with French knots worked using two strands of cotton.

3 Press on the reverse side with a damp cloth.

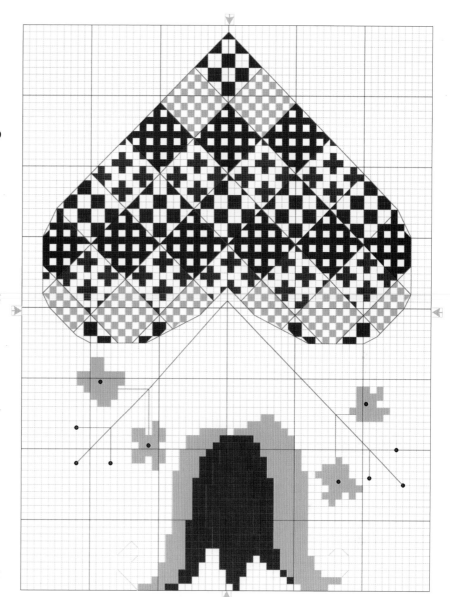

TO MAKE UP

Anchor stranded cotton

CROSS STITCH KEY
Anchor 306
Anchor 1036
Anchor 1028
Anchor 218

BACK STITCH KEY
— Anchor 1028
— Anchor 306

FRENCH KNOT KEY
:: Anchor 1036

1 Stick double-sided tape round the outside edges of the front and back inside covers of the notebook, leaving the protective backing paper attached. Cut the wadding to fit the front and back covers of the book and iron in place.

2 Lay the linen face down with the embroidery on the left-hand side. Stand the book along the cross-ways tacking line and check the cross stitch design will be just above the centre. Drop the front

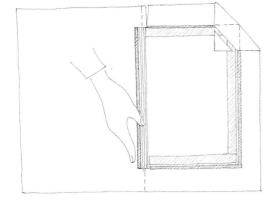

cover flat and trim the linen to about 1½in (4cm) from the edge.

3 Peel off the protective backing paper from the double-sided tape and fold in the corners of the linen. Fold in the side flap, mitring the corners carefully (see page 30). Snip the linen close to the spine of the book, then fold in the top and bottom flaps, again mitring the corners neatly.

4 Close the front cover and repeat the process on the back cover. Make sure that the cover is smooth and isn't pulled too tight otherwise the book won't close properly.

5 Trim half the fabric from the spine tab. Open the book out and tuck the excess fabric down the inside of the spine using a bodkin or large needle. Repeat at the other end.

6 Open the front cover. Stick double-sided tape round the edge of the fly leaf. Remove the backing paper and press down to cover the raw edges of the cover. Repeat inside the back cover to complete.

FRACTUR PICTURE

*A*LONG *with tulips and hearts, birds were a most popular subject in Pennsylvanian folk art. Taken from a fractur bookmark, this unusual design originally featured thirty-six birds. It has been enlarged and simplified to make this beautiful, colourful picture which will give pleasure for years to come.*

MATERIALS

- ❖ 14in (36cm) square of 25-count white evenweave fabric, Anchor FSE25M
- ❖ tacking thread
- ❖ needle
- ❖ Anchor stranded cotton 11, 13, 217, 257, 306, 387, 403, 858, 891, 1034, 1036
- ❖ size 24 tapestry needle
- ❖ 11in (28cm) square of mountboard
- ❖ pencil
- ❖ ruler
- ❖ pins
- ❖ strong thread
- ❖ scissors
- ❖ picture frame

TO STITCH

1 Fold the evenweave in four to find the centre and tack guidelines in both directions.

2 Work the cross stitch from the middle out using two strands of cotton over two threads of linen. Where two colours are stipulated for the same stitch, thread one strand of each colour together in the needle.

3 Work the French knots with two strands and the back stitch with a single strand of cotton.

4 Wash the design with a mild detergent if required and press on the reverse side.

Anchor stranded cotton

CROSS STITCH KEY

■ Anchor 403	◢ Anchor 11	▨ Anchor 387+306
■ Anchor 1036	5 Anchor 387	◿ Anchor 858+306
■ Anchor 1034	▨ Anchor 858	◼ Anchor 1034+217
▨ Anchor 306	7 Anchor 891	
▥ Anchor 13	▨ Anchor 1034+891	BACK STITCH KEY
▨ Anchor 217	▲ Anchor 1034+11	= Anchor 257
▨ Anchor 257	▨ Anchor 387+13	= Anchor 403

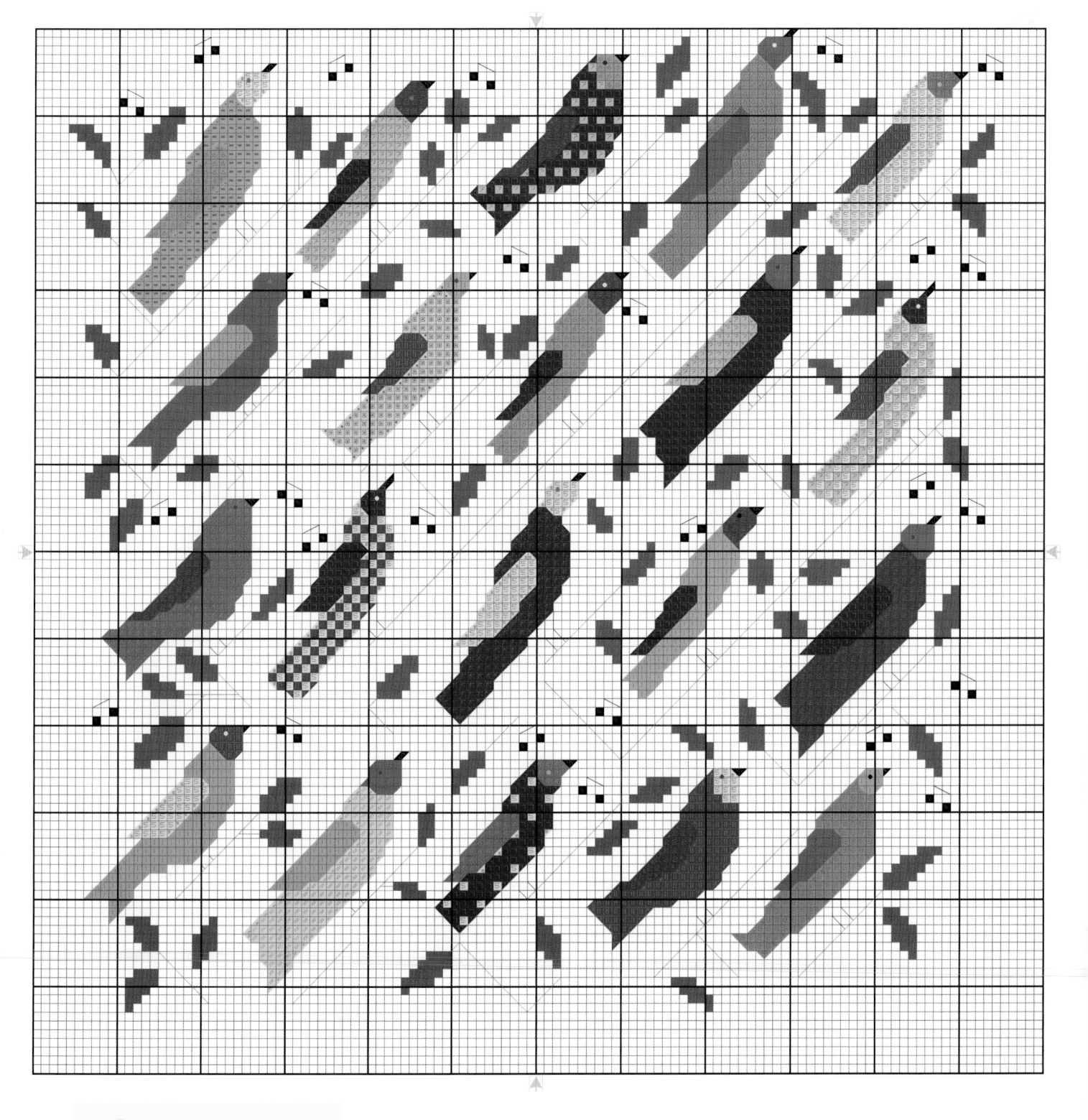

FRENCH KNOT KEY
:: Anchor 403
:: Anchor 1036
:: Anchor 1034
:: Anchor 306
:: Anchor 13
:: Anchor 217
:: Anchor 11
:: Anchor 387

TO MAKE UP

1 Measure the mountboard and mark the centre point on each side. Lay the embroidery face down on a flat surface and position the mountboard on top, matching the centre marks to the tacked guidelines.

2 Stretch the evenweave over the mountboard as shown on page 33 and fit it in a frame of your choice.

BREAD BASKET LINER

*O*NE of the most distinctive folk art traditions of the
Pennsylvanian Dutch was their bright and bold painted
tinware. This attractive scroll border and simple daisy motif
design were originally painted on to a large tin jug.

MATERIALS

❖ 18in (46cm) square of 28-count
golden brown linen, Zweigart
E3281
❖ tacking thread
❖ needle
❖ tape measure
❖ Anchor Nordin flower thread 13,
301, 891
❖ size 24 tapestry needle
❖ tailor's wax (optional)
❖ pins
❖ scissors
❖ sewing thread
❖ 15in (38cm) square of homespun
gingham fabric

TO STITCH

1 Tack a 12in (30cm) square guideline in the middle of the linen.
Work the border design inside the
tacked line using a single thickness
of cotton over two threads of linen.
You may find it easier to stitch
flower thread through linen if each
length is lightly waxed before use.

2 Once the border is complete, count
the threads carefully to position
and stitch the flowers.

3 Press on the reverse side with a
damp cloth.

TO MAKE UP

1 Fold under and press a 1½in (4cm)
hem on the linen. Open out the
hem, then pin and tack the gingham fabric to the reverse side of
the linen, wrong sides together.

2 Mitre the corners of the linen (see
page 30). Fold the raw edge under
¼in (5mm). Refold the hem and
tack in position close to the inside
fold line. Machine stitch on the

fold line. Machine stitch on the
right side close to the tacking
thread. Slip stitch the mitred
corners, remove the tacking thread
and press the piece on the reverse
side to finish.

CROSS STITCH KEY

Anchor Nordin flower thread

▨	Anchor 891
■	Anchor 13
▨	Anchor 301

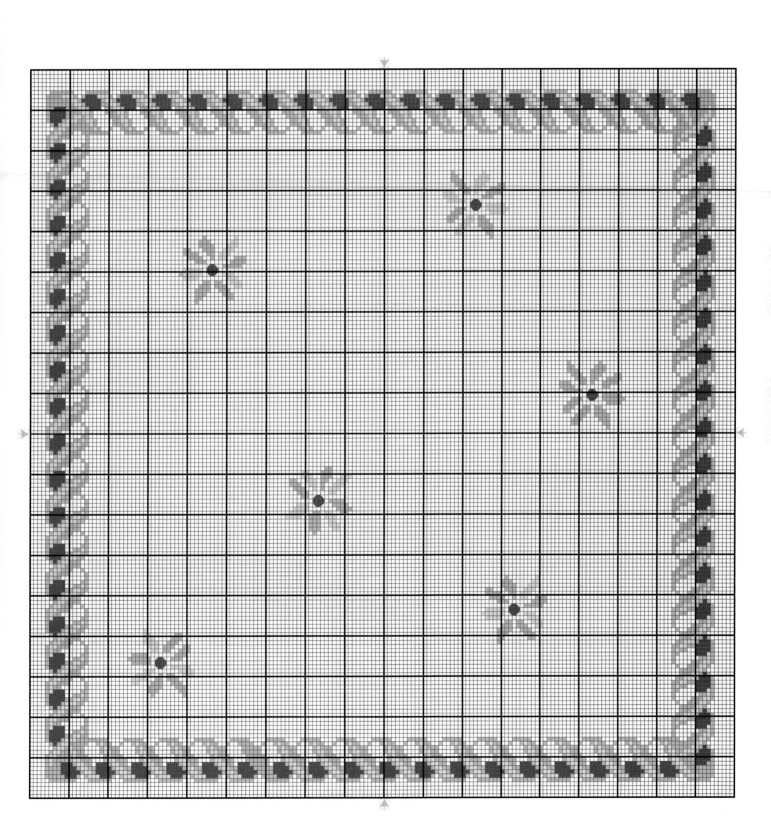

LAVENDER MINI-CUSHION

*THE Amish of Lancaster County made alphabet samplers
which were stored in chests or drawers and used to provide
templates for the family linen. This little heart motif was taken
from one of the earliest known Amish samplers.*

MATERIALS

* 10 x 26in (25 x 66cm)
* 28-count white Cashel linen,
  Zweigart E3281
* graph paper
* pencil
* sewing thread
* two ⅝in (1.5cm) four-hole
  buttons
* two 5in (13cm) squares of 2oz
  (50g) wadding
* lavender sachet
* tailor's wax (optional)
* tape measure
* scissors
* tacking thread
* needle
* Anchor Nordin flower thread 212
* size 24 tapestry needle

TO STITCH

1 Cut a 10 x 16in (25 x 40cm) piece
of linen, leaving the remaining 10in
(25cm) square on one side. Tack a
guideline across the linen rectangle
2½in (6cm) from each end.

2 Work the heart motif in the centre
top of the linen with the bottom of
the motif just touching the guideline. Use a single thickness of flower
thread over two threads of linen.

You may find it easier to stitch flower thread through linen if each length is lightly waxed before use.

3 Select and draw out your initials on a piece of graph paper, leaving one square between the letters. Stitch the initials in the middle above the bottom guideline.

4 Press on the reverse side with a damp cloth.

TO MAKE UP

1 Cut the rectangle in two, 4in (10cm) from each motif. Turn under and stitch a small hem along the cut edge. Fold under a further 1½in (4cm) and press.

2 Make two vertical ⅝in (1.5cm) buttonholes in the heart-motif section, 2in (5cm) apart and ⅝in (1.5cm) from the folded edge. Overlap the embroidered pieces to make a 10in (25cm) square. Pin and tack the layers together.

3 With right sides together, stitch the front and back together, ⅝in (1.5cm) from the edge. Trim across the corners, trim the seams and turn through.

4 Ease out the corners and press on the reverse side. Tack a guideline 1¼in (3cm) in from the edge and, working inside the line, stitch single cross stitches through the top layer of linen only.

5 Once complete, machine stitch through both layers just inside the cross stitches. Sew a button behind each of the buttonholes using a decorative cross stitch.

6 Tuck the lavender sachet between the layers of wadding and insert into the cushion cover. Fasten the buttons to complete.

Anchor Nordin flower thread

CROSS STITCH KEY
■ Anchor 212

AMISH QUILT GREETINGS CARDS

*A*MISH quilts are uniquely identifiable. The colours are always dark, but strong design and unusual colour combinations produce stunning results as shown here in the classic Centre Diamond and Double Nine Patch designs.

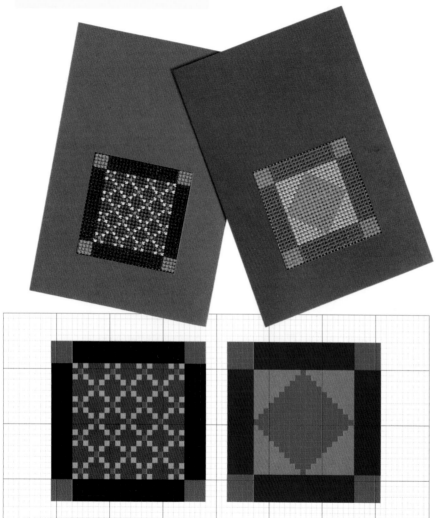

MATERIALS

DESIGN 1
❖ 5in (13cm) square of red stitching paper, Inglestone Collection
❖ Anchor stranded cotton 13, 164, 1039
❖ 4¼ x 6in (11 x 15cm) black double-fold craft card

DESIGN 2
❖ 5in (13cm) square of green stitching paper, Inglestone Collection
❖ Anchor stranded cotton 13, 403, 858, 862
❖ 4¼ x 6in (11 x 15cm) dark green double-fold craft card
❖ size 24 tapestry needle
❖ scissors
❖ pencil
❖ safety ruler
❖ craft knife
❖ cutting mat
❖ double-sided tape

TO STITCH

1 Work each design in the middle of the stitching paper using two strands of cotton. Take the needle up and down through the paper carefully to prevent it tearing. If necessary the paper can be repaired using sticky tape and the holes repunched using a large needle.

TO MAKE UP

1 Measure the size of the cross stitch panel. Open out the card flaps and mark the size of the aperture on the wrong side of the centre panel. Have an equal border width above and to each side of the aperture.

2 Cut along the pencil lines carefully with a sharp knife. Trim the stitching paper to ½in (12mm) all round and position over the aperture. Overlap the edges of the stitching paper with double-sided tape. Peel off the backing paper and press the left flap down securely to complete the card.

CROSS STITCH KEY

Anchor stranded cotton

▨	Anchor 164
▨	Anchor 13
▨	Anchor 858
▨	Anchor 403
▨	Anchor 862
▨	Anchor 1039

SUNSHINE AND SHADOW
PIN CUSHION

YOU *can tell an Amish household by the dark green blinds
and this little pin cushion uses the colour to great effect. The
sunshine and shadow quilt block, with colours shading out from
dark into light, was developed by the Amish in the nineteenth
century and is now immensely popular all over America.*

MATERIALS

- ❖ 4in (10cm) square of 16-count
  smoky green Aida, Zweigart 3251
- ❖ DMC flower thread 2319, 2320,
  2369, 2715, 2890
- ❖ size 26 tapestry needle
- ❖ scissors
- ❖ pins
- ❖ two 6in (15cm) squares of dark
  green velvet
- ❖ sewing thread
- ❖ needle
- ❖ polyester wadding

TO STITCH

1 Work the design using a single
thickness of flower thread.

2 Once complete, press on the
reverse side and trim to within ¼in
(5mm) of the cross stitch.

TO MAKE UP

1 Fold under the excess Aida and pin
the cross stitch panel in the middle
of one piece of velvet. Slip stitch
round the edge securely.

2 With right sides facing, sew the
velvet squares together, leaving a
gap along one side. Trim the seams
and across the corners and turn
through. Stuff firmly with wadding
and slip stitch the gap to finish.

DMC flower thread

CROSS STITCH KEY

▨ DMC 2319
▨ DMC 2320
■ DMC 2890
☐ DMC 2715
▨ DMC 2369

STRAWBERRY HERB PLANTER

*T*HE *Pennsylvanian Dutch settlers painted all sorts of household objects in their bold and simple style. This bright strawberry motif was adapted from a design originally painted on the lid of a wooden candle box.*

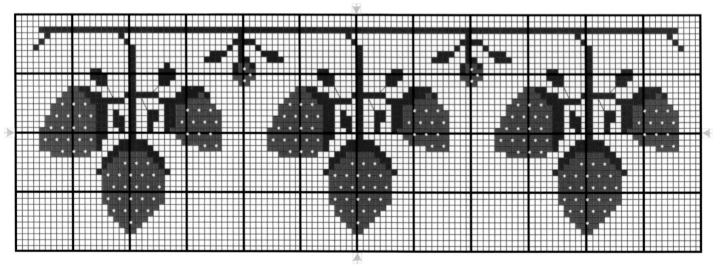

MATERIALS

❖ 24in (61cm) of 3½in (9cm) wide white woven-edge Aida band, Zweigart E7316
❖ masking tape
❖ tape measure
❖ pins
❖ scissors
❖ Anchor Nordin flower thread 217, 926, 9046
❖ size 24 tapestry needle
❖ bare wood planter
❖ green reproduction paint, Colourman 108
❖ paint brush
❖ medium wire wool
❖ small tacks
❖ hammer

TO STITCH

1 Wrap the Aida band round the planter until it is fairly taut and tape the ends down on the back. Measure along the front of the planter and mark the centre with a pin. Mark the centre of each side panel in the same way.

2 Begin the middle strawberry motif four holes down from the woven border and work the cross stitch using a single thickness of flower thread. Don't take the thread across the back of this band between motifs because it will show through on the right side.

3 Stitch the small strawberry motif 17 holes down from the woven border. Work all the French knots as shown.

4 Press on the reverse side.

TO MAKE UP

1 Paint the planter and allow to dry. Rub along the edges with wire wool to distress the edges and wipe away any dust with a damp cloth.

2 Turn under ½in (12mm) at each end of the Aida band. Use the masking tape to fix the band temporarily in position, then hammer in several small tacks to secure on the back of the planter. Remove the masking tape.

Anchor Nordin flower thread

CROSS STITCH KEY
■ Anchor 9046
■ Anchor 217

BACK STITCH KEY
— Anchor 217

FRENCH KNOT KEY
❀ Anchor 926

GRAPEVINE SHELF BORDER

*S*EWING *was an essential skill among Amish women who valued the tools of their trade. This grapevine motif, originally painted on a cherished Amish button box, may well have been inspired by a popular quilting pattern from the 1930s.*

MATERIALS

- ❖ 3in (7.5cm) wide scalloped-edge white linen band, Zweigart E7312, 39 stitches
- ❖ tape measure
- ❖ scissors
- ❖ Anchor stranded cotton 13, 44, 217, 1036
- ❖ size 24 tapestry needle
- ❖ double-sided tape

TO STITCH

1 Measure the shelf and work out how many repeats need to be stitched bearing in mind that each repeat measures approximately 10in (25cm).

2 Cut the linen band 2in (5cm) longer than the shelf to allow for turnings. Fold the band in half crossways to find the centre. If there are an odd number of repeats, begin in the centre of the design; if there are an even number of repeats, begin at the end of the design.

3 To stitch the design centrally on the linen, leave a space of four threads of linen above the middle leaf. Work the cross stitch using two strands of cotton over two threads of linen. Where two colours are

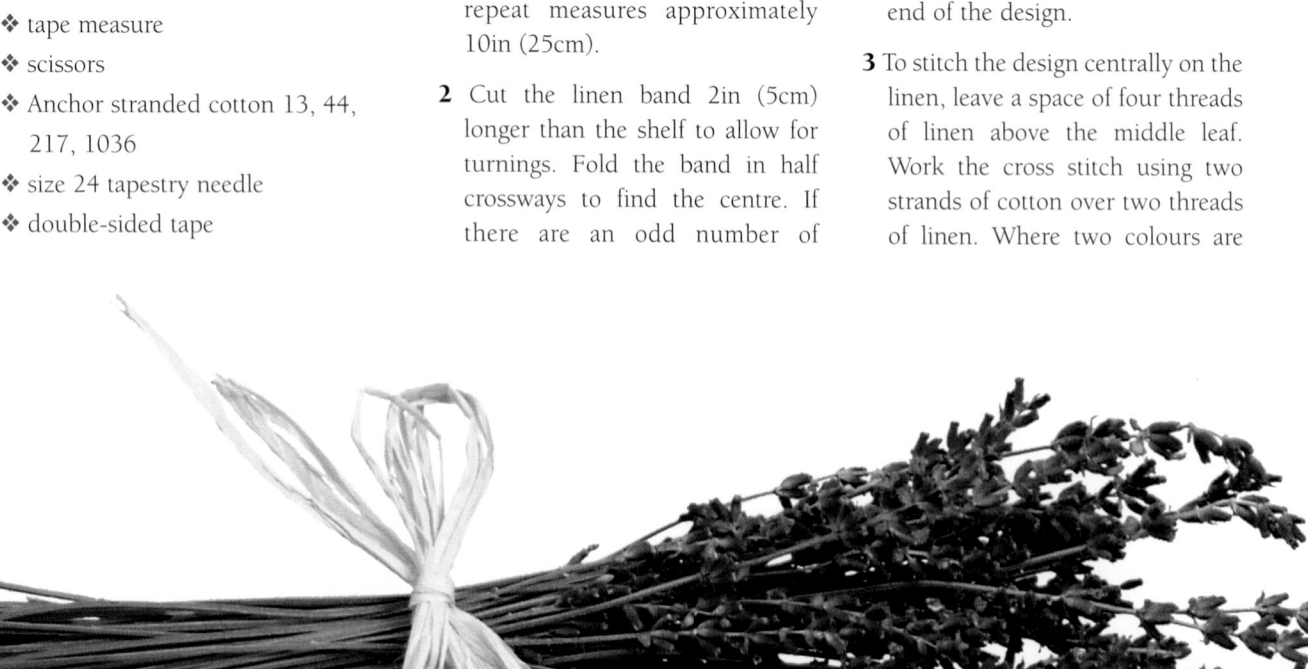

TO MAKE UP

Anchor stranded cotton

CROSS STITCH KEY
■ Anchor 1036
■ Anchor 13+44
■ Anchor 217
■ Anchor 44
■ Anchor 13

BACK STITCH KEY
▨ Anchor 1036

1 Measure the shelf and turn under the ends of the linen band to fit. Use double-sided tape to stick the band to the front of the shelf.

stipulated, use a single strand of each colour together in the needle.

4 Once the cross stitch is complete, work the back stitch using a single strand of cotton.

5 Press on the reverse side with a damp cloth.

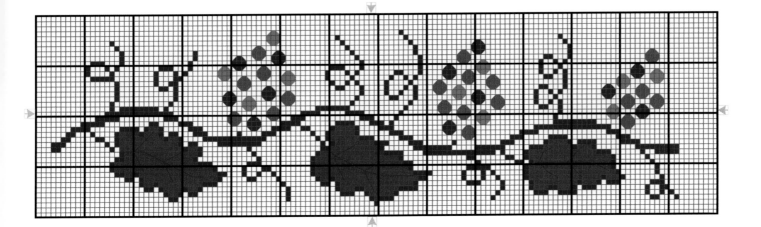

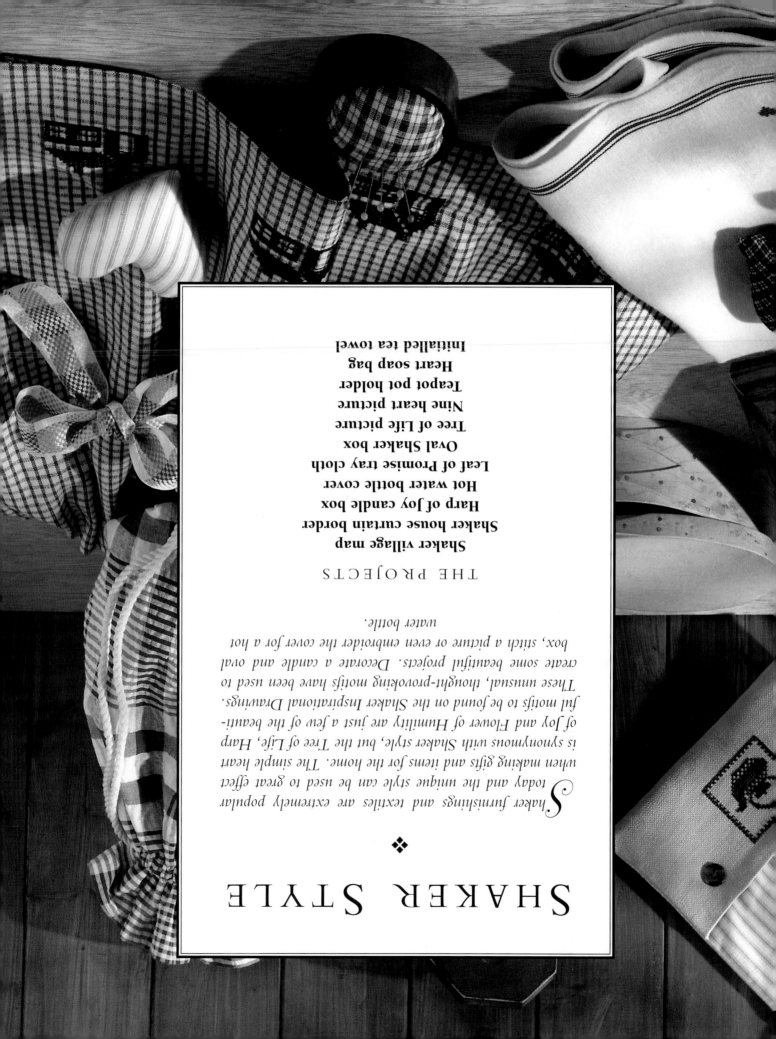

SHAKER STYLE

❖

Shaker furnishings and textiles are extremely popular today and the unique style can be used to great effect when making gifts and items for the home. The simple heart is synonymous with Shaker style, but the Tree of Life, Harp of Joy and Flower of Humility are just a few of the beautiful motifs to be found on the Shaker Inspirational Drawings. These unusual, thought-provoking motifs have been used to create some beautiful projects. Decorate a candle and oval box, stitch a picture or even embroider the cover for a hot water bottle.

THE PROJECTS

Shaker village map
Shaker house curtain border
Harp of Joy candle box
Hot water bottle cover
Leaf of Promise tray cloth
Oval Shaker box
Tree of Life picture
Nine heart picture
Teapot pot holder
Heart soap bag
Initialled tea towel

SHAKER VILLAGE MAP

*T*HE *wash house, large meeting rooms and little houses on this design are laid out in an unusual Shaker style. Drawn in a naïve way, part of the map is upside down and some houses even seem to sprout from the roofs of others.*

MATERIALS

❖ 14in (36cm) square of 27-count white evenweave, Anchor FSE27M

❖ tacking thread

❖ needle

❖ Anchor stranded cotton 20, 47, 133, 150, 257, 302, 306, 335, 351, 403, 862, 921, 936

❖ size 24 tapestry needle

❖ scissors

❖ 12 x 10in (30 x 25cm) mount-board

❖ ruler

❖ pencil

❖ pins

❖ strong thread

❖ picture frame

TO STITCH

1 Fold the linen in four and tack guidelines across the centre in both directions. Begin 2in (5cm) down from the top of the even-weave. Work the cross stitch border first using two strands of cotton over two threads of linen.

2 Checking the position carefully (it isn't central), back stitch the cross road using a single strand of cotton. This will reduce the design areas and make it easier to count threads and stitch the house outlines in the correct positions.

Anchor stranded cotton

CROSS STITCH KEY
■ Anchor 47
■ Anchor 20
■ Anchor 302
■ Anchor 306
■ Anchor 862
■ Anchor 257
■ Anchor 150
■ Anchor 351
■ Anchor 936
■ Anchor 133
■ Anchor 921

BACK STITCH KEY
— Anchor 862
— Anchor 351
— Anchor 403

FRENCH KNOT KEY
∷ Anchor 335
∷ Anchor 302
∷ Anchor 862
∷ Anchor 257

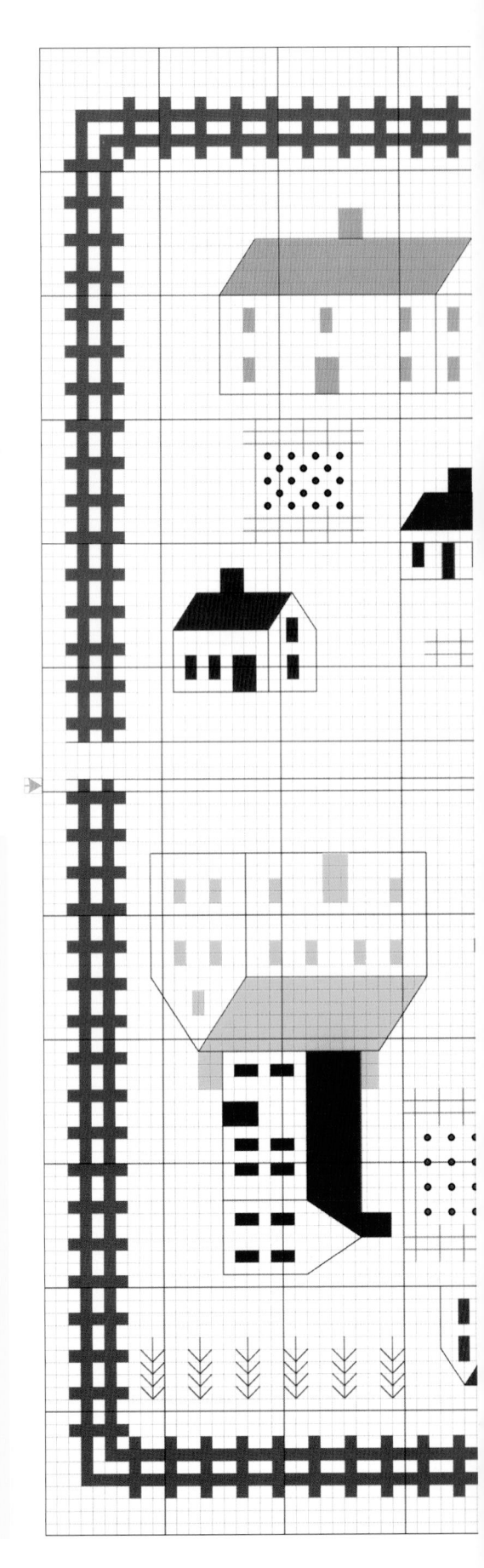

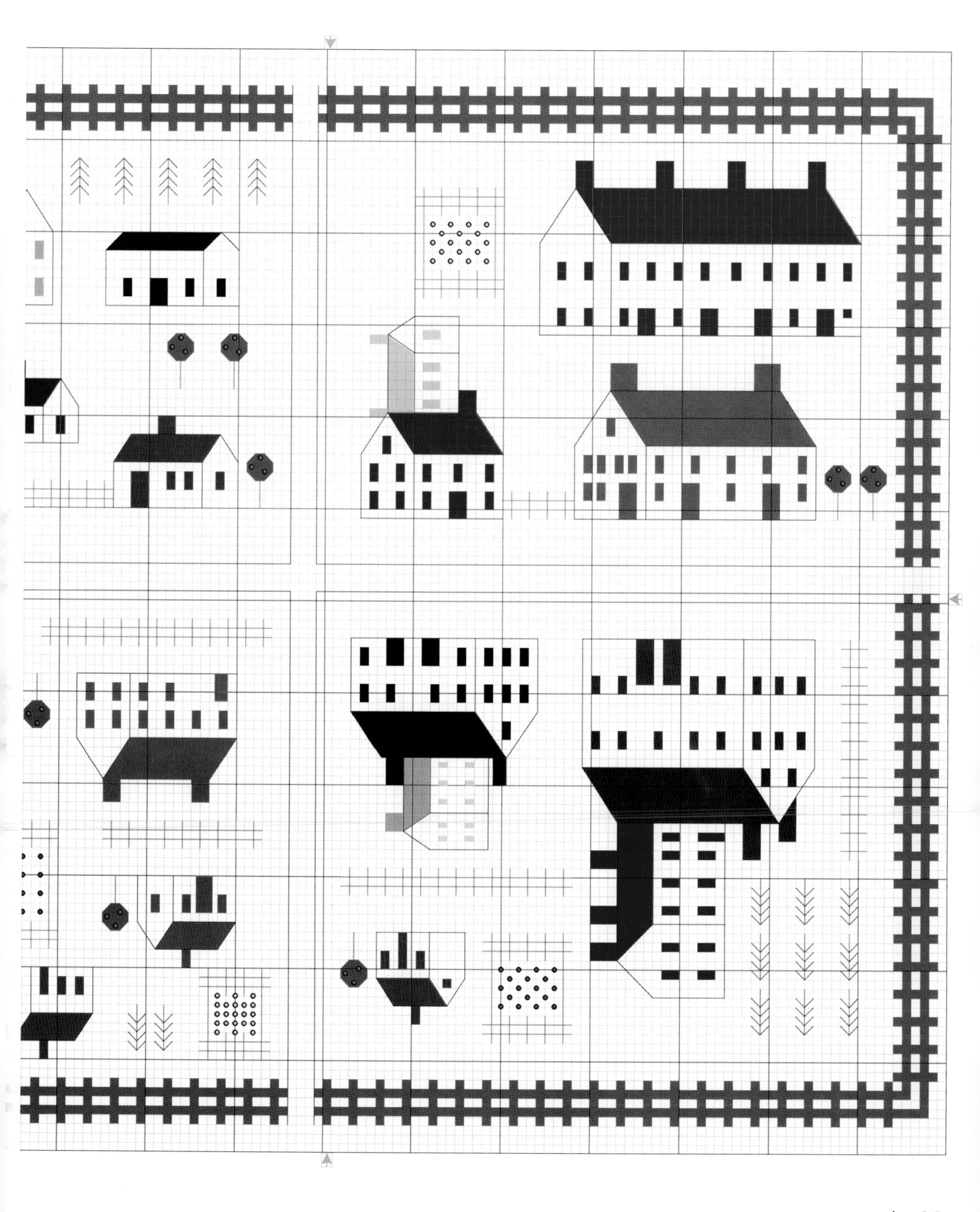

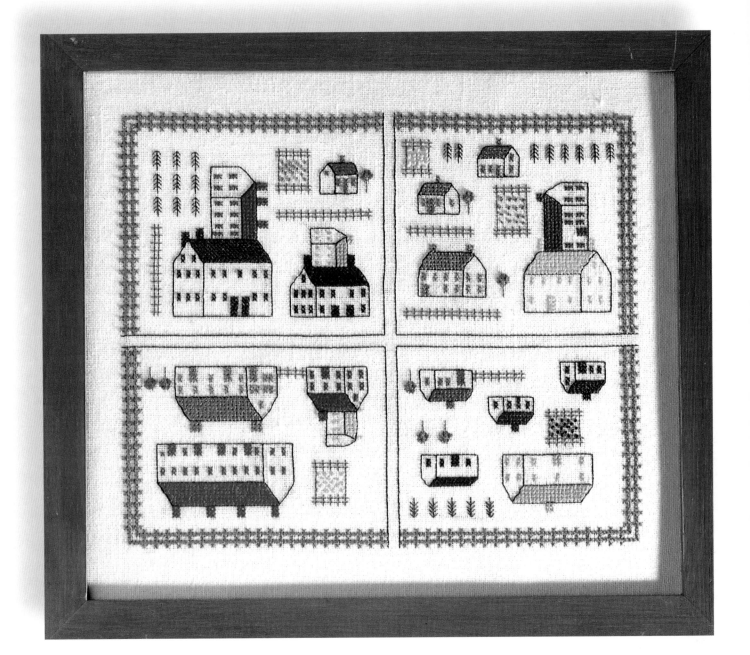

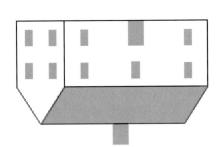

TO MAKE UP

1 Measure the mountboard and mark the centre point on each side. Lay the embroidery face down on a flat surface and position the mountboard on top, matching the centre marks to the tacked guidelines.

2 Stretch the evenweave over the mountboard as shown on page 33 and fit it in a frame of your choice.

3 Cross stitch the windows, doors and roofs, filling in any bare areas of roof space with half cross stitches.

4 Finally stitch the fences, fields and trees, working the French knots with two strands of cotton.

5 Press on the reverse side when complete.

SHAKER HOUSE CURTAIN BORDER

*'W*HATEVER *is fashioned, let it be plain and simple and for the good.' The simplicity of Shaker architecture is reflected in this dwelling house motif adapted from a nineteenth-century appliqué quilt.*

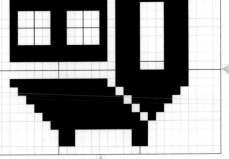

Anchor nordin flower thread

CROSS STITCH KEY
■ Anchor 127

BACK STITCH KEY
═ Anchor 127

MATERIALS

- ❖ gingham curtain fabric (twice the width of the window by the window drop plus 6in (15cm) for turnings)
- ❖ scissors
- ❖ sewing thread
- ❖ tape measure
- ❖ pins
- ❖ tacking thread
- ❖ needle
- ❖ 10-count waste canvas
- ❖ Anchor Nordin flower thread 127 (one skein for every four motifs)
- ❖ size 24 tapestry needle
- ❖ tailor's wax (optional)
- ❖ curtain heading tape

TO STITCH

1 Sew lengths of fabric together to make the required width of curtain and press the seams open. Tack a guideline 6in (15cm) up from the bottom edge. Allowing for side turnings, mark the position of the motifs, spacing the pins about 4½in (11.5cm) apart.

2 Tack 3 x 4in (7.5 x 10cm) pieces of waste canvas at each pin above the tacking line. Work the motifs using a single thickness of flower thread, taking care to make the cross stitches as even as possible. You may find it easier to run the flower thread through the tailor's wax before stitching.

3 Once the motifs are complete, remove the tacking thread and begin to fray the canvas. Pull the threads out one at a time using a pair of tweezers for grip if required.

TO MAKE UP

1 Fold up a 4in (10cm) hem along the bottom edge and slip stitch in position.

2 Turn under ¼in (5mm) down the side seams and machine stitch close to the fold. Turn under a further 1in (2.5cm) and press with a damp cloth.

3 Turn under ¼in (5mm) along the top edge and stitch curtain heading to the reverse side to complete.

4 Press on the reverse side with a damp cloth.

HARP OF JOY CANDLE BOX

MATERIALS

❖ 10in (25cm) of 2¾in (7cm) wide linen band, 31 stitches

❖ tape measure

❖ DMC stranded cotton 518, 676, 781, 3765

❖ size 24 tapestry needle

❖ scissors

❖ candle box blank

❖ yellow and dark blue reproduction paints, Colourman 102, 104

❖ paint brush

❖ medium steel wool

❖ clear beeswax

❖ double-sided tape

TO STITCH

1 Measure down 2¾in (7cm) from the top of the linen band and stitch the blue heart in the centre using two strands of cotton over two threads of linen.

2 Complete the remaining cross stitch. Work the curved back stitch on either side of the harp with two strands of cotton. All other back stitch is worked with a single strand.

3 Work the French knots with two strands of cotton to complete the harp design.

4 Press on the reverse side with a damp cloth.

TO MAKE UP

1 Paint the candle box with yellow paint and allow to dry. Paint a coat of blue on top.

2 When this is dry, rub gently down the edges and over the corners of

*T*HE *Harp of Joy is a motif inspired by Mother Ann Lee who told the Shakers to 'provide places for all your things, so that you may know where to find them at any time, day or night'. This practical candle box serves such a purpose and can be hung from a peg rail in true Shaker style.*

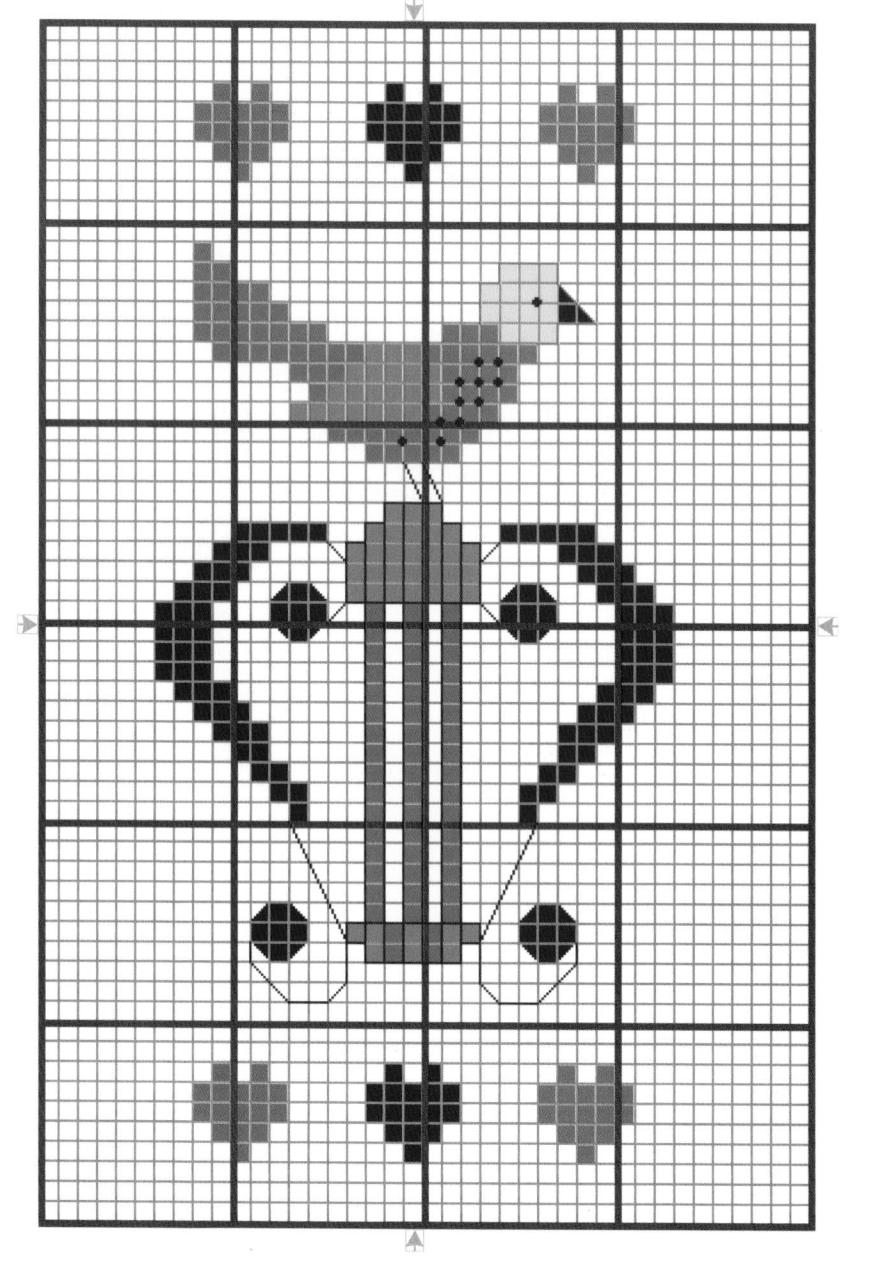

the box until the yellow paint begins to show through. Wipe off any dust with a damp cloth and apply a coat of beeswax.

3 Position the motif in the middle of the front panel. Use double-sided tape to stick the ends inside and underneath the box.

DMC stranded cotton

CROSS STITCH KEY
◼ DMC 781
◼ DMC 3765
▫ DMC 676
◼ DMC 518

BACK STITCH KEY
▭ DMC 3765
▭ DMC 781

FRENCH KNOT KEY
▓ DMC 3765

HOT WATER BOTTLE COVER

MATERIALS

- 13¾ x 17½in (35 x 45cm) 25-count cream evenweave, Anchor FSE25M
- Anchor stranded cotton 301, 306, 879, 897
- size 24 tapestry needle
- scissors
- hot water bottle
- paper
- pencil
- 36in (91cm) square of red, green and cream gingham fabric
- 12 x 36in (30 x 91cm) light-weight wadding
- pins
- sewing thread
- 36in (91cm) red cord

TO STITCH

1 Fold the evenweave in half lengthways to mark the centre line. Measure up 8in (20cm) from the bottom to find the centre point of the cross stitch.

2 Work the cross stitch using three strands of cotton over two threads of linen. Work the French knot flower centres and the bird's eye.

3 Press on the reverse side with a damp cloth.

TO MAKE UP

1 Draw round the edge of the hot water bottle adding 1¼ in (3cm) down the sides and along the bottom. Add 2in (5cm) round the top and neck. Fold the paper in half lengthways and trim to make the sides symmetrical.

*T*HE *Shakers have some delightful sayings recorded in the Inspirational Paintings. While stitching this beautiful heart-shaped floral wreath surrounding the Dove of Peace, think about this simple motto: 'Hands to work and Hearts to God'.*

2 Cut three pattern pieces out of gingham and two out of the lightweight wadding. Position the pattern piece on the evenweave so that the design is just above the centre and cut it out. Layer one piece of wadding between two pieces of gingham and the other between the evenweave and gingham.

3 Tack the layers together ⅜in (1.5cm) from the edge and trim the seam allowance to ⅜in (9mm).

4 Cut several 1½in (4cm) bias strips from the remainder of the gingham (see page 30). Join the strips together to fit round both the front and back covers.

5 Pin and stitch the bias strip along the seam line on the right side. Turn the bias strip under ⅜in (9mm) and fold over to the reverse side. Slip stitch in place.

6 Cut two 1½in (4cm) strips of fabric to fit across the neck. Turn under and stitch a small hem at each end then turn under ⅜in (9mm) on each long side. Pin and stitch across the neck to form the casing. With reverse sides facing, pin the front and back covers together, then stitch along the bottom and up the sides next to the bias binding.

7 Fold a 4in (10cm) length of cord in half and stitch securely on the inside, at the top of the right-hand side seam. Cut the remaining cord in half and thread one piece through each side of the casing. Tie an overhand knot about 2in (5cm) from each end. Unravel the cord to form simple tassels. Trim the ends, insert the hot water bottle and tie the ends together in a bow.

Anchor stranded cotton

CROSS STITCH KEY
Anchor 301
Anchor 879
Anchor 897
Anchor 306

FRENCH KNOT KEY
:: Anchor 897
:: Anchor 306

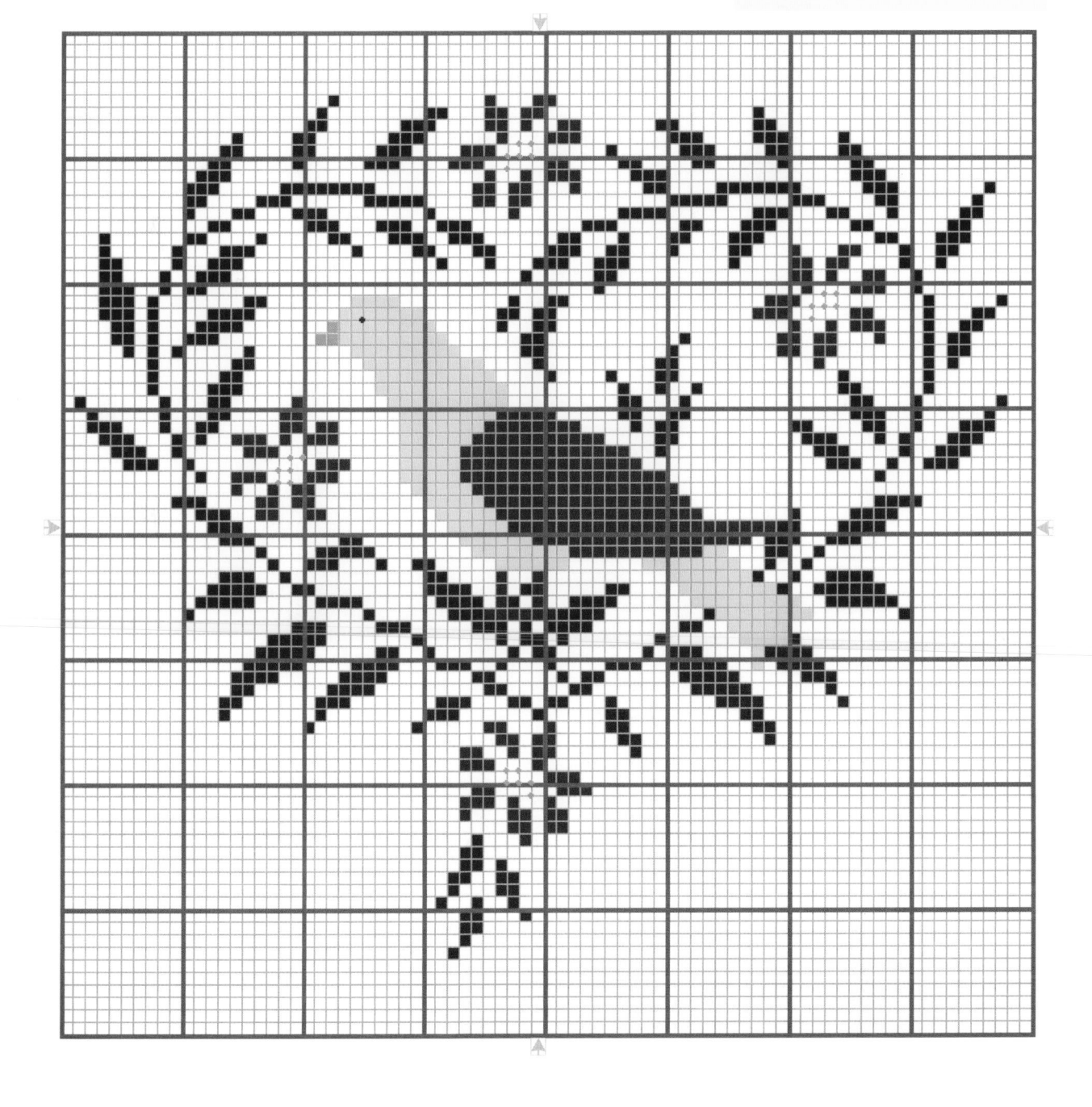

LEAF OF PROMISE
TRAY CLOTH

*A simple tray covered with this beautifully embroidered tray
cloth is the perfect accompaniment for breakfast in bed or a
quiet supper by the fire, and the aptly named Leaf of Promise
from Shaker Inspirational art, the ideal motif.*

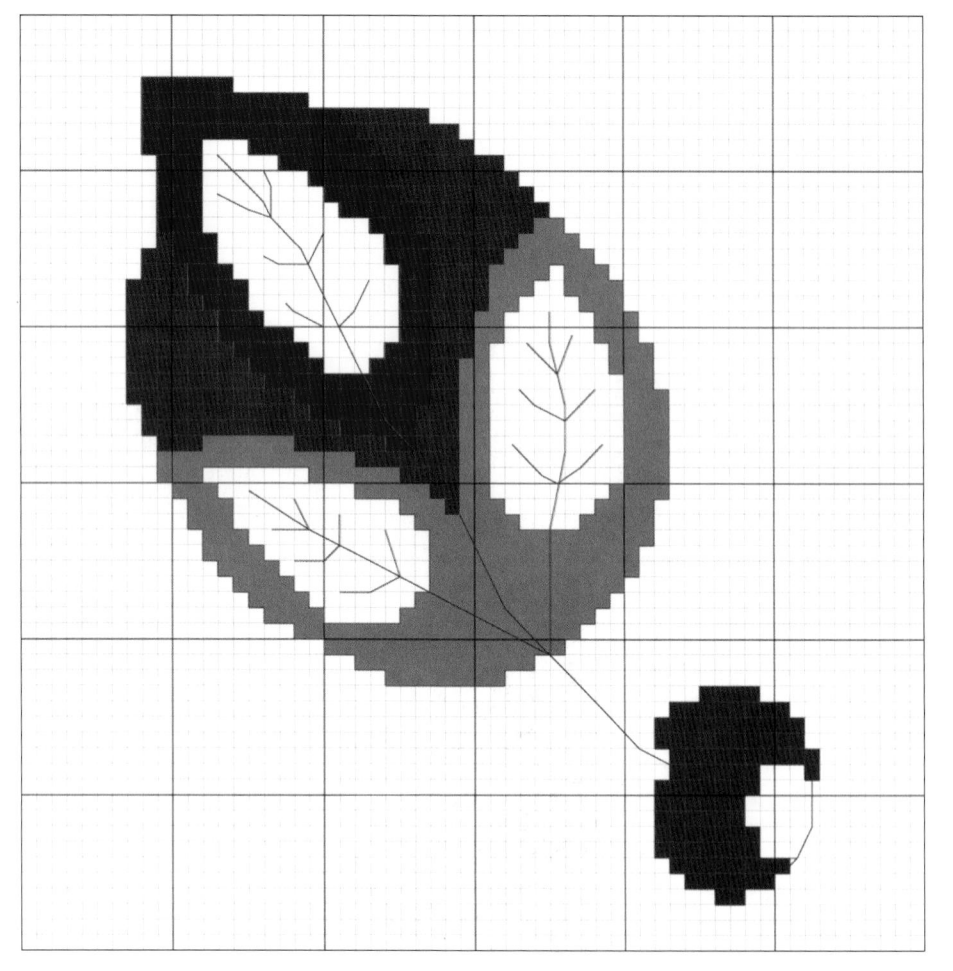

MATERIALS

- 28-count sage green Quaker
  cloth, Zweigart E3993
- tape measure
- tacking thread
- needle
- size 24 tapestry needle

- Anchor Nordin flower thread
  218, 897, 920
- tailor's wax (optional)
- scissors
- sewing thread

Anchor Nordin flower thread

CROSS STITCH KEY
- ■ Anchor 920
- ■ Anchor 897
- ■ Anchor 218

BACK STITCH KEY
- ═ Anchor 897
- ═ Anchor 218

TO STITCH

1 Add 3in (7.5cm) to the inside measurements of the tray to allow for turnings and cut the linen accordingly. For example, if the tray measures 12 x 15in (30 x 38cm), cut the linen 15 x 18in (38 x 46cm).

2 Tack a guideline round one corner 2¾in (7cm) in from each side. This marks the bottom right-hand corner of the cross stitch design.

3 Work the cross stitch and the back stitch using a single thickness of flower thread. You may find it easier to run the flower thread through the tailor's wax before stitching.

4 Press on the reverse side with a damp cloth.

TO MAKE UP

1 Measure out 1¼in (3cm) from the tacked guideline. Fold the linen under along the straight grain and press each side in turn. Press an equal hem on the other two sides.

2 Open out and trim the turnings to 1¼in (3cm). Mitre the corners (see page 30), turn the raw edge under ¼in (5mm) and tack the hem close to the fold.

3 Machine stitch on the right side close to the tacking thread. Slip stitch the mitred corners on the reverse side and press with a damp cloth to finish.

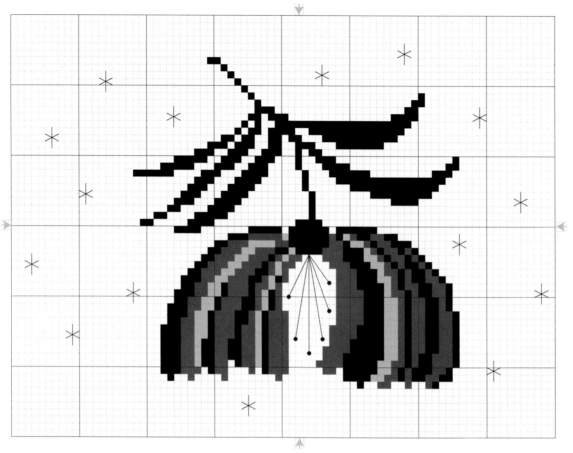

OVAL SHAKER BOX

***T**HE distinctive Shaker box made with faultless craftsmanship encapsulates the old belief that 'Beauty rests on utility'. Decorated with the Flower of Humility, this box can be used for storing embroidery threads or other sewing equipment.*

MATERIALS

- ❖ 7in (18cm) long Shaker box with lid
- ❖ 8 x 10in (20 x 25cm) 27-count cream evenweave, Anchor FSE27C
- ❖ Anchor stranded cotton 152, 891, 922
- ❖ size 24 tapestry needle
- ❖ 5 x 7in (13 x 18cm) iron-on wadding
- ❖ pencil
- ❖ scissors
- ❖ double-sided tape
- ❖ 20in (50cm) of ¾in (2cm) wide cream ribbon
- ❖ dark blue reproduction paint, Colourman 104
- ❖ black acrylic paint
- ❖ paint brush
- ❖ medium wire wool

TO STITCH

1 Fold the linen in four to find the centre point and work the flower motif using two strands of cotton over two threads of linen.

2 Back stitch the flower stamens using two strands of cotton and the small stars with a single strand.

3 Press on the reverse side with a damp cloth.

Anchor stranded cotton

CROSS STITCH KEY
- ▨ Anchor 891
- ■ Anchor 152
- ▨ Anchor 922

BACK STITCH KEY
- ▬ Anchor 152

FRENCH KNOT KEY
- :: Anchor 152

TO MAKE UP

1 Lay the box lid on top of the wadding, draw round and cut out along the marked line. Iron the wadding in place on top of the lid and fit on to the box.

2 Position the cross stitched linen on top of the lid and press down all round to make a crease showing the shape. Cut round ½in (12mm) outside the crease line.

3 Stick a strip of double-sided tape round the rim of the lid and remove the backing paper. Reposition the cross stitched linen, smoothing the edges down on to the tape.

4 Stick a second layer of double-sided tape round the rim. Fold under the end of the ribbon and stick round the rim. Trim the other

end to fit allowing for a small turning and stick down securely.

5 Paint the base of the Shaker box with dark blue paint. (Mix some black acrylic paint into the blue reproduction paint if required.)

6 Rub down the paint lightly until the brass tacks show through to complete the box.

TREE OF LIFE PICTURE

As the Shaker movement began to decline towards the mid nineteenth-century, artists looked to the past for inspiration. This Tree of Life was drawn as a gift to the North family from their spiritual leader, Mother Anna Lee.

MATERIALS

❖ 14 x 15in (36 x 38cm)
  27-count white evenweave,
  Anchor FSE27L
❖ tacking thread
❖ needle
❖ DMC stranded cotton 300, 700,
  702, 726, 780, 3348, 3765
❖ size 24 tapestry needle
❖ 10 x 11in (25 x 28cm)
  mountboard
❖ pins
❖ strong thread
❖ picture frame

TO STITCH

1 Fold the linen in four to find the centre and tack guidelines across in both directions.

2 Work the cross stitch using two strands of cotton over two threads of linen. Where two colours are specified for the same stitch, work a single strand of each colour together in the needle.

3 Work the back stitch using a single strand of cotton.

4 Wash the embroidery in a mild detergent if required and press on the reverse side.

TO MAKE UP

1 Measure the mountboard and mark the centre point on each side. Lay the embroidery face down on a flat surface and position the mountboard on top, matching the centre marks to the tacked guidelines.

2 Stretch the evenweave over the mountboard as shown on page 33 and fit into a frame of your choice.

CROSS STITCH KEY

DMC stranded cotton

■ DMC 780+300
■ DMC 702
■ DMC 700
■ DMC 3348
□ DMC 726
■ DMC 3765

BACK STITCH KEY

= DMC 700

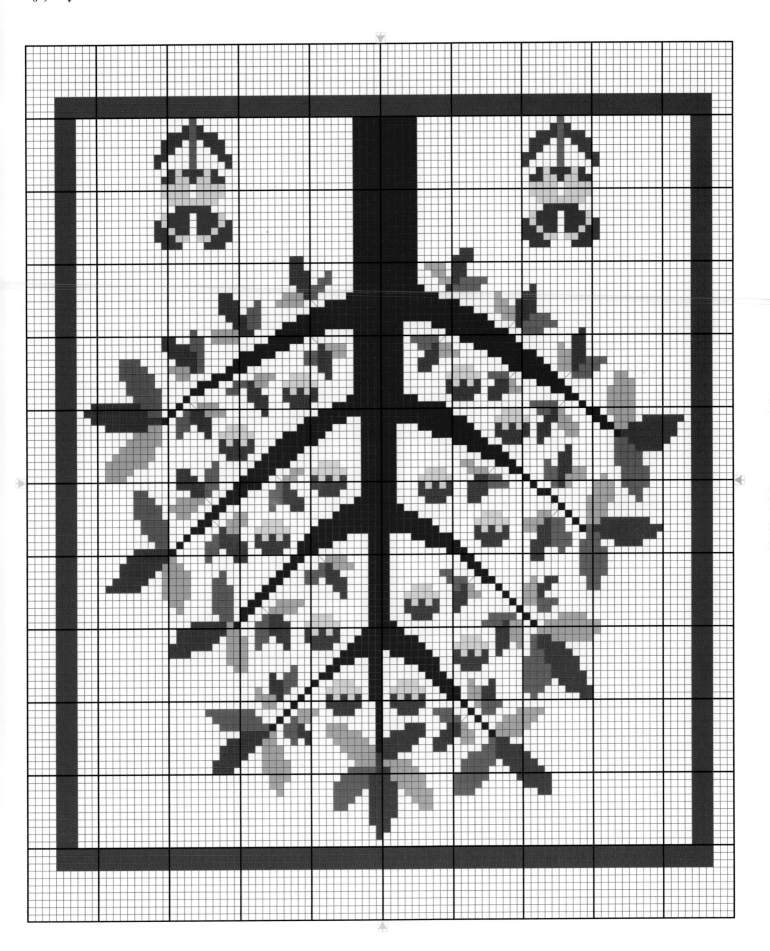

H OMESPUN gingham fabrics were favoured by the Shakers for their
simplicity and practicality. This pretty picture can be given as gift
inscribed with a rhyming message like this inspirational motto: 'Look
at this and think of me, your loving Mother Anna Lee.'

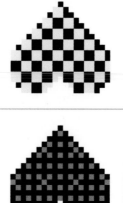

CROSS STITCH KEY

Anchor stranded cotton

☐	Anchor 386
	Anchor 133
	Anchor 335
	Anchor 47
	Anchor 20
⊠	Anchor 302
	Anchor 267
	Anchor 257
	Anchor 149
	Anchor 936
	Anchor 921
⊙	Anchor 265
⊡	Anchor 343

BACK STITCH KEY

—	Anchor 267
—	Anchor 265

FRENCH KNOT KEY

∷	Anchor 257

MATERIALS

❖ 14 x 15in (36 x 38cm) 28-count antique white Cashel linen, Zweigart E3281
❖ tacking thread
❖ needle
❖ Anchor stranded cotton 20, 47, 133, 149, 257, 265, 267, 302, 335, 343, 386, 921, 936
❖ size 24 tapestry needle
❖ 6¼in (16cm) square of mount-board
❖ ruler
❖ pencil
❖ strong thread
❖ picture frame

TO STITCH

1 Fold the linen in four to find the centre point and tack guidelines across the centre in both directions.

2 Work the centre heart using two strands of cotton over two threads of linen.

3 Back stitch the squares with a single strand of cotton and then stitch the remaining hearts.

4 Press on the reverse side with a damp cloth.

TO MAKE UP

1 Measure the mountboard and mark the centre point on each side. Lay the embroidery face down on a flat surface and position the mountboard on top, matching the centre marks to the tacked guidelines.

2 Stretch the evenweave over the mountboard as shown on page 33 and fit in a frame of your choice.

TEAPOT POT HOLDER

SIMPLE cotton fabrics and a delightful teapot motif have been used to make this practical pot holder that combines the Shaker ideals of form and function. Tuck a message or recipe card under the flap if it is to be given as a gift.

MATERIALS

- ❖ 7 x 10in (18 x 25cm) 28-count sand Quaker cloth, Zweigart E3993
- ❖ tape measure
- ❖ Anchor Nordin flower thread 22, 905
- ❖ size 24 tapestry needle
- ❖ tailor's wax (optional)
- ❖ pins
- ❖ tacking thread
- ❖ needle
- ❖ sewing thread
- ❖ 7 x 10in (18 x 25cm) yellow / white stripe fabric
- ❖ 10 x 16in (25 x 40cm) yellow gingham
- ❖ tailor's chalk
- ❖ safety pin or bodkin
- ❖ 10in (25cm) square of heavy-weight calico
- ❖ 10in (25cm) square of 2oz (50g) wadding
- ❖ two ⅝in (1.5cm) four-hole buttons

TO STITCH

1 Fold the linen in half crossways to mark the centre line and open out. Measure 2¾in (7cm) up from the bottom edge and mark the centre point of the cross stitch motif.

2 Work the design using a single thickness of flower thread over two threads of linen. Press on the reverse side with a damp cloth.

You may find it easier to stitch flower thread through linen if each length is lightly waxed before use.

TO MAKE UP

1 Turn under the top raw edge ¼in (5mm) and machine stitch. Neaten the bottom long edge of the stripe fabric in the same way. Lay the stripe fabric right side up. Fold the linen over to the reverse side, ¾in (2cm) above the cross stitch motif. Position on top of the stripe fabric to make a 10in (25cm) square and tack the pieces together down the sides.

2 Cut a 10in (25cm) square from the gingham. Cut a 1½in (4cm) bias strip from the left-over fabric. Press the strip to remove some of the stretch and fold in half lengthways with right sides together. Stitch ½in (12mm) from the fold, turn through using a safety pin or bodkin, then press.

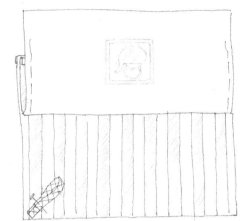

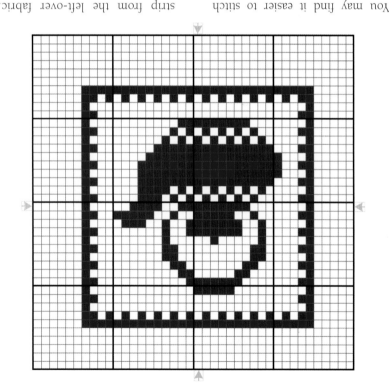

6 Sew a button on either side of the cross stitch motif about 4in (10cm) apart, stitching through all layers to complete. Insert your fingers inside the front flap to make it easy to grab a pot handle.

Anchor Nordin flower thread

CROSS STITCH KEY
■ Anchor 22
■ Anchor 905

5 Trim the wadding to fit inside the pad and insert through the flap on the front. Make sure the wadding is flat and reaches right into all the corners.

4 Lay the check fabric square on top with right sides together and then the calico square. Pin, tack and machine round all sides. Trim the seams in layers to reduce bulk and trim across the corners before turning through. Ease out the corners and press.

3 Trim the bias tube to 4in (10cm) and fold in half crossways. Pin diagonally in the top right hand corner of the front panel with the loop facing in. Tack securely.

HEART SOAP BAG

MATERIALS

- ❖ 18 x 21in (46 x 53cm) burgundy seersucker, Fired Earth Shaker patchwork
- ❖ Anchor Nordin flower thread 926
- ❖ size 24 tapestry needle
- ❖ tailor's wax (optional)
- ❖ sewing thread
- ❖ tape measure
- ❖ scissors
- ❖ 13 x 21in (33 x 53cm) cotton lining
- ❖ 1⅔ yds (1.5m) size 4 piping cord
- ❖ tea
- ❖ safety pin or bodkin

TO STITCH

1 The heart motif can be stitched directly on to the checks of the fabric if the squares are even and measure about 10 to 1in (2.5cm). Otherwise work the cross stitch over a suitable square of 10-count waste canvas.

2 Stitch the heart in the centre of the fabric about 6in (15cm) up from the bottom edge. Using a single thickness of flower thread, work the stitches as evenly as possible and press on the reverse side when complete. You may find it easier to stitch flower thread through the fabric if each length is lightly waxed before use.

TO MAKE UP

1 With right sides together, stitch the back seam and press open with the seam running down the centre back. Stitch along the bottom edge and press the seam open. Open out the corner, line the bottom seam up with the side seam and

STITCHED with a plain heart motif and made from traditional American seersucker fabric, this practical and roomy soap bag has been designed with regard for the Shaker belief in simplicity, utility and durability.

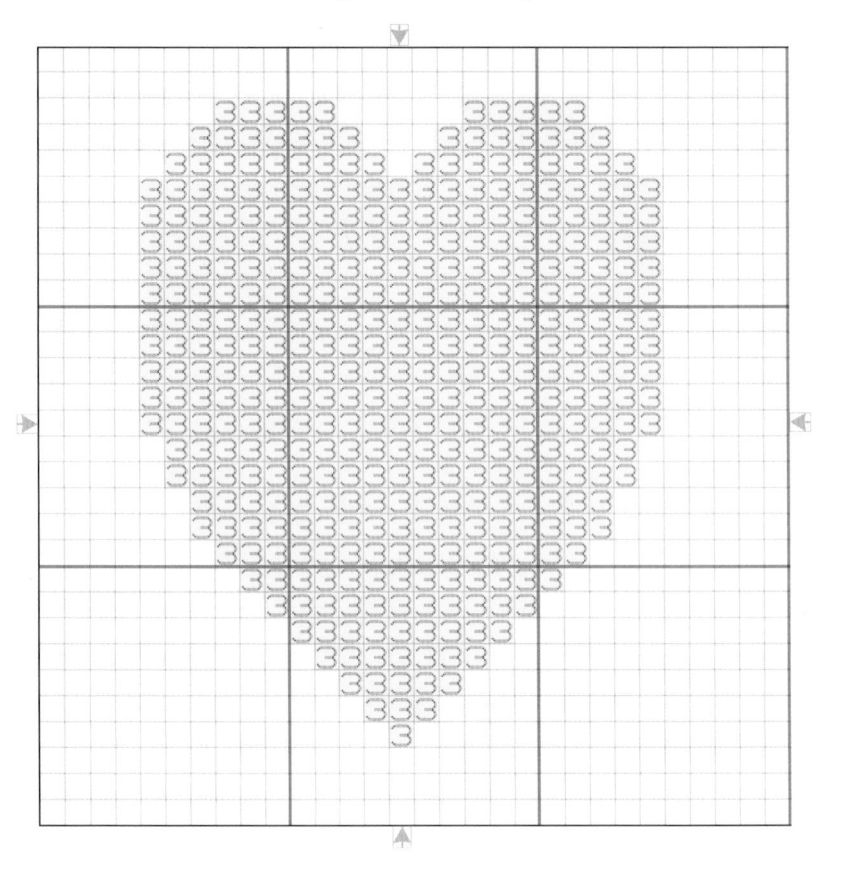

hold in position with a pin. Measure 1¾in (4.5cm) down from the corner and pin. Tack and machine along the marked line. Trim off the excess fabric and save the pieces to make the cord tabs.

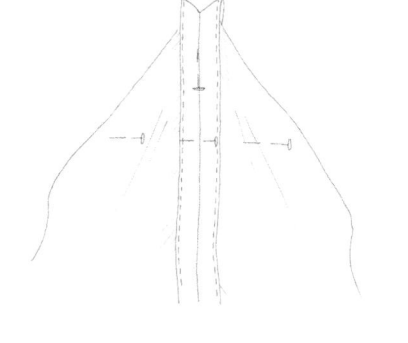

Anchor Nordin flower thread

CROSS STITCH KEY
☒ Anchor 926

2 Turn through to the right side. Measure 9½in (24cm) up each side seam and stitch a ½in (12 mm) vertical buttonhole above the mark. Cut the buttonholes carefully with a pair of sharp scissors. Make up the lining in the same way, but without the buttonholes, and leave wrong-side out.

3 Slip the lining inside the seersucker bag matching the back seams and pin in place from the outside. Fold the top edge of the seersucker over the lining to make a 3in (7.5cm) hem on the inside. Fold under the raw edge ¼in (5mm) and tack in position, catching the lining inside the hem.

4 Stitch a 1in (2.5cm) casing by stitching through all layers on either side of the buttonholes.

5 Dip the piping cord in tea to colour slightly and cut in half when it is dry. Using a safety pin or bodkin, thread one length through the casing and back out the same buttonhole. Thread the second piece through the other buttonhole in the same way.

6 Sew across the saved corner pieces to make two ¾ x 1½in (2 x 4cm) tabs. Trim the seams and across the corners and turn through. Ease out the corners, tuck the raw edges inside and press. Slip the ends of the cords inside the tabs and stitch securely across the top.

INITIALLED TEA TOWEL

*I*N *the Shaker community there was a communal wash house for laundry and 'public cupboards' for spare clothes and linen. All household linen was marked with the name of the family and clothes with the wearer's initials. Stitch your own initials or family name in the corner of a linen towel or bed linen.*

MATERIALS

- ❖ tea towel
- ❖ graph paper
- ❖ pencil
- ❖ 14-count waste canvas
- ❖ tacking thread
- ❖ DMC stranded cotton 824
- ❖ size 24 tapestry needle

TO STITCH

1 Draw out the name or initials you want to stitch on graph paper. Space the letters carefully, leaving two spaces between straight-sided letters and one or even possibly no space if next to wide diagonal letters. Draw in the dots and hearts to complete the motif which should look evenly spaced as a whole.

2 Work out the size of the cross stitch using 14 stitches to 1in (2.5cm) and cut a piece of waste canvas at least 1in (2.5cm) larger. Tack in position at the bottom of the tea towel. Work the cross stitch using a two strands of cotton.

3 Once the stitching is complete, begin to fray the waste canvas. Pull the threads out one at a time, using tweezers if required.

4 Press on the reverse side with a damp cloth once all the canvas threads have been removed.

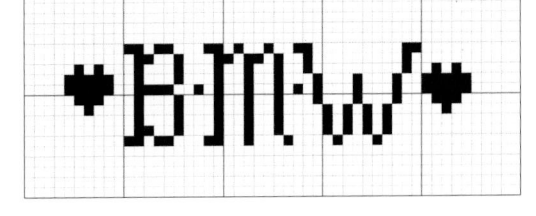

DMC stranded cotton

CROSS STITCH KEY
■ DMC 824

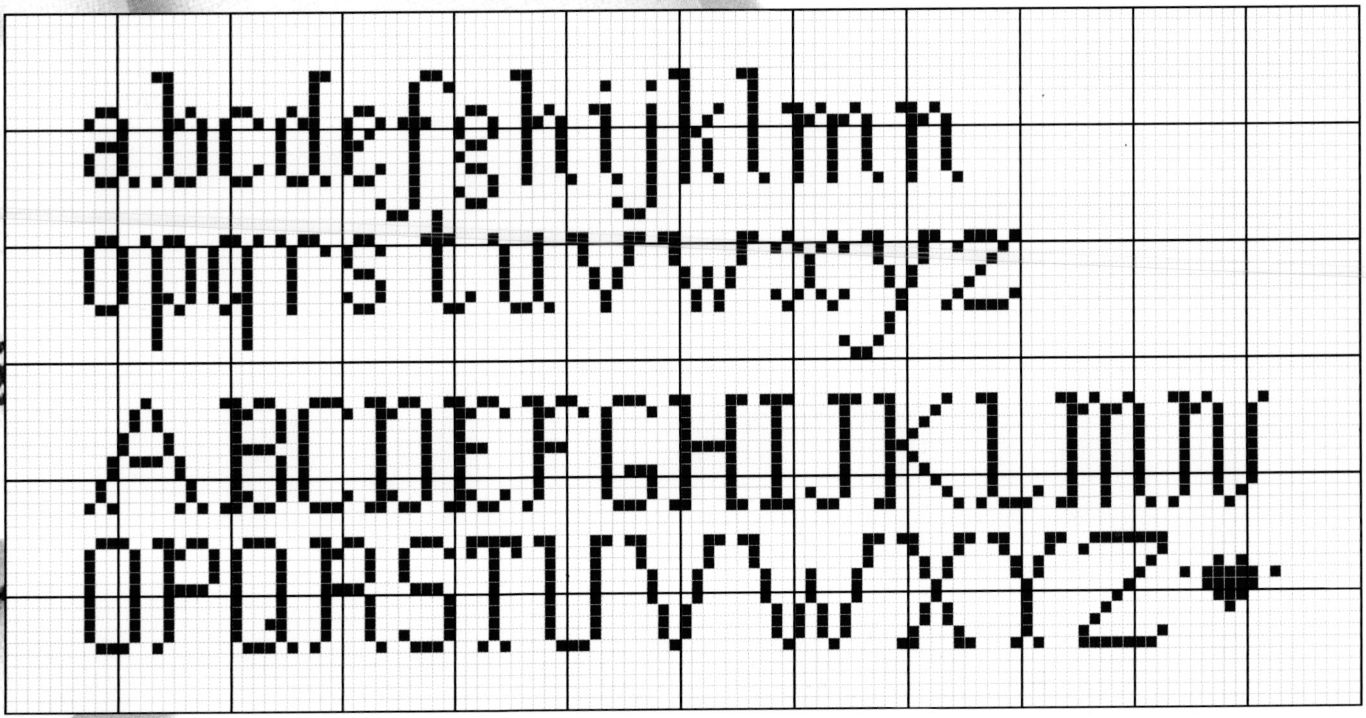

NEW ENGLAND
INSPIRATIONS

❖

The New England settlers decorated their homes and furnishings with few resources. Stencilling was a cheap way to transform their floors and furniture, while the scraps of fabric they collected were used to make exquisite appliqué quilts and colourful hooked rugs. All these handicrafts feature simple and colourful plant forms, birds, animals and tropical fruits that can be worked to great effect in cross stitch. Try stitching a quirky cockerel on a cushion or stitch a stencil design to make into an attractive clock.

THE PROJECTS

Star shoe bag
Folk art door panel
Heart pillowcase border
Mulberry clock
Baltimore quilt cushion
Salt box
Leafy table mat
Cockerel cushion
Flower pot picture
Linen tie-backs

STAR SHOE BAG

*E*VER *resourceful, most colonial households saved every remnant of cloth to make into pieced quilts and one of the most popular motifs was the star. As the settlers moved west, new stars like this Ohio star were created to celebrate territories officially becoming States.*

MATERIALS

- ❖ 17 x 23in (43 x 59cm) 32-count antique blue Belfast linen, Zweigart E3609
- ❖ sewing thread
- ❖ tape measure
- ❖ graph paper
- ❖ pencil
- ❖ DMC stranded cotton 518, 815, 991, 993, 3328, 3765
- ❖ size 26 tapestry needle
- ❖ pins
- ❖ 1⅓ yds (1.25m) of ⅜in (9mm) wide red double satin ribbon
- ❖ tacking thread
- ❖ needle
- ❖ safety pin or bodkin

TO STITCH

1 Neaten the raw edges of the linen with overlocking or machine zigzag.

2 Select the initials required from the chart and draw them out on graph paper leaving two squares between each letter. Mark the centre point.

3 Measure 6in (15cm) in from the left-hand side and 5in (13cm) up from the bottom edge to find the centre point of the cross stitch. Stitch the initials first using two strands of cotton over two threads of linen.

4 Count the threads carefully to space and stitch the patchwork motifs.

5 Press on the reverse side with a damp cloth.

TO MAKE UP

1 Fold the linen in half crossways with the design on the inside. Measure 4in (10cm) down the side seam and mark with a pin. Insert another pin 1in (2.5cm) further down to show the position of the casing for the ribbon.

2 Stitch along the bottom and up the side, leaving a gap between the pins. Sew in the thread ends securely and press the seams open. Turn through to the right side and ease out the corners.

3 Fold over a 2in (5cm) hem along the top edge. Turn the raw edge under ¼in (5 mm) and pin. Tack and machine stitch through all layers on either side of the gap on the side seam to form a 1in (2.5cm) wide casing.

4 Machine buttonhole for ½in (12mm) across the top and bottom of the gap for extra strength.

5 Thread the ribbon in through the gap and round the casing, using a safety pin or bodkin. Keep going right round again and pull the ends level. Tie the ribbons together near the end with an overhand knot and trim diagonally to complete.

DMC stranded cotton

C R O S S S T I T C H K E Y
- ■ DMC 991
- ■ DMC 815
- ■ DMC 518
- ■ DMC 3765
- ■ DMC 993
- ■ DMC 3328

FOLK ART DOOR PANEL

THE *classic combination of bird, heart and tulips found in folk art all over the world come together in this delightful cross stitch design inspired by a panel in a traditional Baltimore friendship quilt.*

MATERIALS

- ❖ 10in (25cm) square of 28-count light tan Cashel linen, Zweigart E3281
- ❖ tacking thread
- ❖ Anchor stranded cotton 152, 301, 306, 308, 879
- ❖ size 24 tapestry needle
- ❖ 6in (15cm) square of mountboard (approx.)
- ❖ craft knife
- ❖ pencil
- ❖ safety ruler
- ❖ double-sided tape
- ❖ small cupboard with 6in (15cm) door panel (approx.)

TO STITCH

1 Fold the linen carefully in four and tack guidelines across the centre in both directions. Work the cross stitch using two strands of cotton over two threads of linen. The tulips are stitched with one strand of each colour used together in the needle.

2 Work the back stitch with a single strand of cotton and the French knots with two strands.

3 Press on the reverse side with a damp cloth.

TO MAKE UP

1 Cut the mountboard to fit inside the cupboard door panel. Measure and mark the centre point on each side. Stick double-sided tape round the edge of the mountboard.

2 Lay the embroidery face down on a flat surface and position the mountboard on top with the centre marks to the tacked guidelines and remove the backing paper from the tape.

3 Stretch the linen over the mountboard, mitring the corners carefully (see page 30). Use double-sided tape to stick the cross stitch panel to the cupboard door to complete.

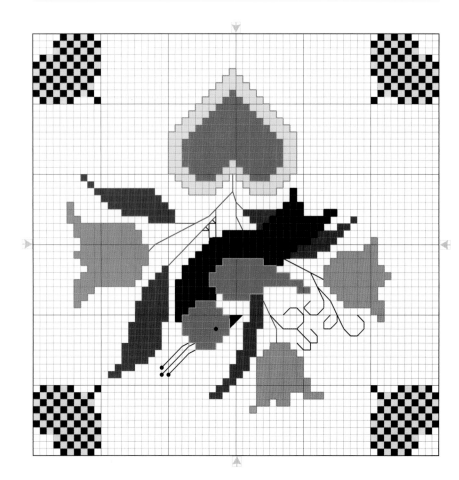

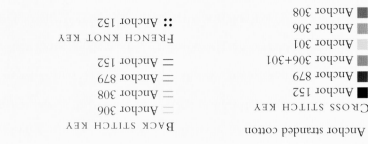

Anchor stranded cotton

CROSS STITCH KEY
Anchor 152
Anchor 879
Anchor 306+301
Anchor 301
Anchor 306
Anchor 308

BACK STITCH KEY
— Anchor 306
— Anchor 308
— Anchor 879
— Anchor 152

FRENCH KNOT KEY
∷ Anchor 152

HEART
PILLOWCASE
BORDER

THE heart is with out doubt the most popular folk art motif of all. This romantic pillowcase edging was inspired by the exquisite crochet lace made by New Englanders to embellish plain towels and bed linen.

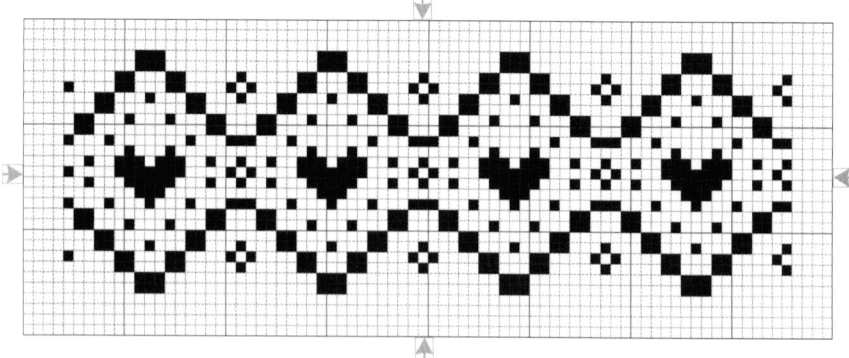

MATERIALS

- ❖ 2in (5cm) wide white scalloped-edge linen band, Zweigart E7311, 23 stitches
- ❖ pillowcase
- ❖ tape measure
- ❖ pins
- ❖ DMC stranded cotton 103
- ❖ size 24 tapestry needle
- ❖ tacking thread
- ❖ needle
- ❖ sewing thread
- ❖ scissors

DMC stranded cotton

CROSS STITCH KEY
■ DMC 103

TO STITCH

1 Check the width of the pillowcase and cut the linen band 2in (5cm) longer. Insert pins in the band to show the approximate length of the cross stitching.

2 Fold the band in half crossways and begin stitching in the centre

using two strands of cotton over two threads of linen. The thread is variegated and can be cut into lengths of light, medium and dark blue before stitching or worked in a more random fashion. Work the design just beyond the pins.

3 Press on the reverse side with a damp cloth.

TO MAKE UP

1 Pin the linen band across the front of pillowcase. Trim the excess band to leave a ⅝in (1.5cm) seam allowance and turn this under. Tack and machine stitch through the front only close to the edge of the linen band.

MULBERRY CLOCK

*C*OLOURFUL *stencilling was very popular among the New Englanders who were determined to make their homes bright and comfortable. Walls, floors and counterpanes were stencilled with quite complex patterns like this pretty floral design.*

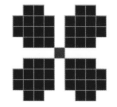

MATERIALS

❖ 12in (30cm) square of 32-count mulberry Belfast linen, Zweigart E3609
❖ tacking thread
❖ needle
❖ Anchor stranded cotton 118, 123, 940, 1028
❖ size 26 tapestry needle
❖ 7in (18cm) square of mountboard
❖ 10in (25cm) square of MDF
❖ 10mm drill
❖ pencil
❖ ruler
❖ pins
❖ strong thread
❖ 40in (102cm) of 1⅜in (3.5cm) wide architrave
❖ mitre saw
❖ wood glue
❖ G-clamps or masking tape
❖ sandpaper
❖ paint
❖ paint brush
❖ clock mechanism

TO STITCH

1 Tack guidelines across the linen in both directions to mark the centre.

2 Work the cross stitch using two strands of cotton over two threads of linen.

3 Press on the reverse side with a damp cloth when complete.

TO MAKE UP

1 Draw two diagonal lines at right angles across the MDF base board to find the centre point. Drill a 10mm hole in the centre of the MDF and another in the middle of the mountboard.

2 Measure the mountboard and mark the centre point on each side. Lay the embroidery face down on a flat surface and position the mount-board on top, matching the centre marks to the tacked guidelines. Stretch the linen over the mount-board as shown on page 33.

Anchor stranded cotton

CROSS STITCH KEY

■ Anchor 1028
■ Anchor 123
■ Anchor 940
■ Anchor 118

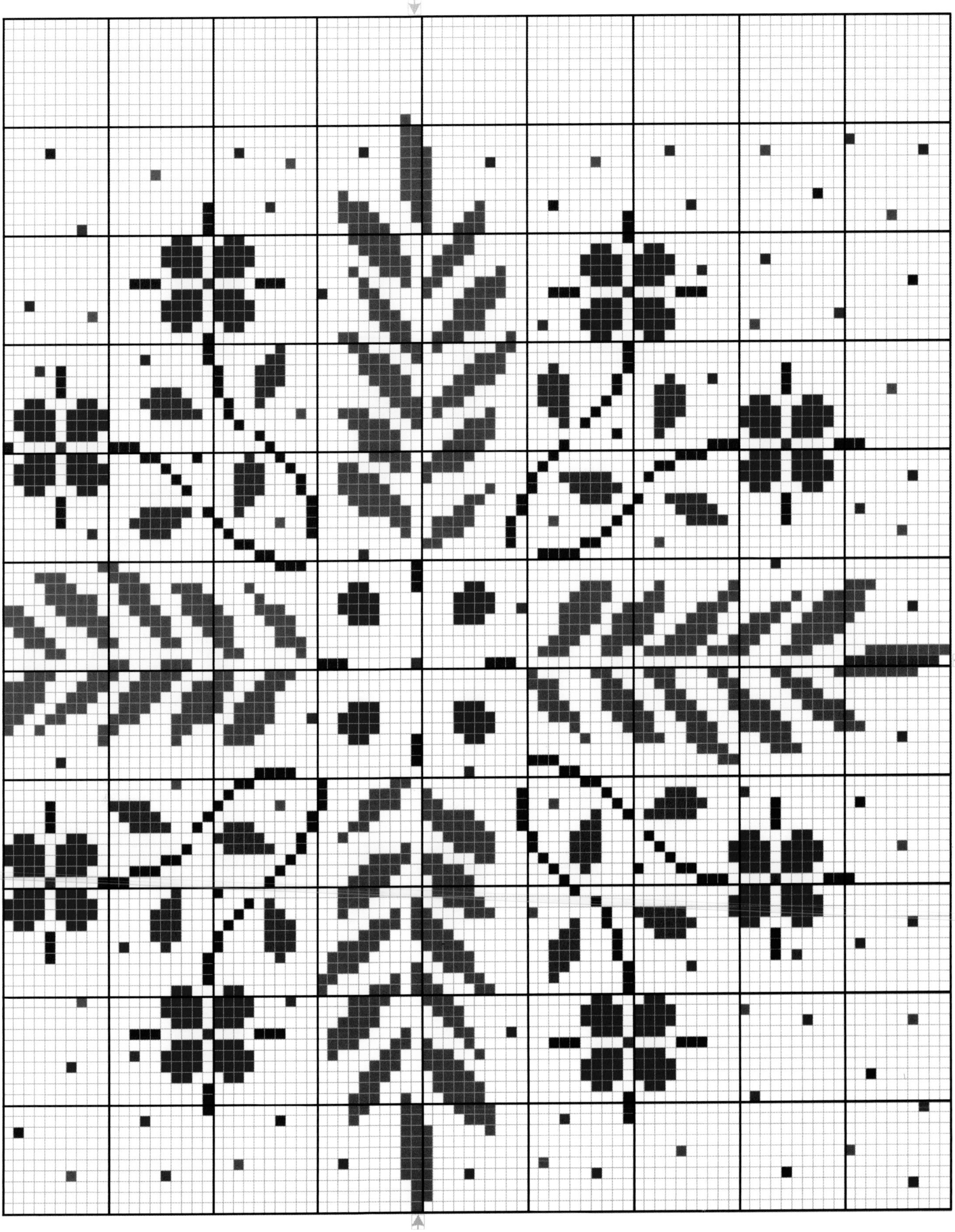

3 Cut the architrave in four equal pieces and mitre the ends. The inside measurement should be the same as the edge of the covered mountboard. Glue the pieces on to the MDF base board, secure with clamps or masking tape and allow to dry.

4 Sand the edges of the MDF flush with the architrave. Paint the frame with two coats of paint. Allow to dry. Paint the hands of the clock to match the frame.

5 Glue the cross stitch panel inside the frame. Snip a few linen threads in the centre of the clock face and fit the clock mechanism as shown in the manufacturer's instructions.

BALTIMORE QUILT CUSHION

*I*N the nineteenth century, album or friendship quilts became popular as women endeavoured to make friends in their new homeland. They would get together in groups and each contribute a square to a quilt. This colourful and complex fruit design shows why Baltimore became the centre of excellence for appliqué quilt making.

MATERIALS

❖ 18in (46cm) square of 28-count cream Cashel linen, Zweigart E3281
❖ tacking thread
❖ needle
❖ DMC stranded cotton, two skeins of 304, one skein each of 90,

300, 349, 353, 472, 500, 523,
666, 676, 700, 702, 727, 780,
817, 995, 3047, 3348, 3362,
3363, 3802, 3808
❖ size 24 tapestry needle
❖ 18in (46cm) of 36in (90cm) wide berry-coloured canvas

❖ scissors
❖ ruler
❖ tailor's chalk
❖ 1¾ yds (1.6 m) size 4 piping cord
❖ pins
❖ sewing thread
❖ 16in (40cm) cushion pad

DMC stranded cotton

CROSS STITCH KEY
■ DMC 666
■ DMC 349
⊞ DMC 349+700
■ DMC 304
■ DMC 3802
5 DMC 3348
6 DMC 472
▨ DMC 700
= DMC 727
▩ DMC 3348+700
▨ DMC 523+500
◼ DMC 3808+995
◹ DMC 90
■ DMC 666+304
⊞ DMC 817
↓ DMC 353
▨ DMC 780+300
■ DMC 780
◙ DMC 300
▲ DMC 3802+304
⊡ DMC 3047+676
▨ DMC 3047
◩ DMC 3362+3047
▷ DMC 702
◙ DMC 3362
▥ DMC 523
▨ DMC 3363
▤ DMC 3362+500
◪ DMC 500
▨ DMC 995
◆ DMC 995+304
■ DMC 995+3802

BACK STITCH KEY
— DMC 300
— DMC 780
— DMC 780+300
— DMC 727
— DMC 500
— DMC 700
— DMC 817

FRENCH KNOT KEY
:: DMC 300
:: DMC 780

TO STITCH

1 Tack guidelines in both directions across the centre of the linen. Work the design using two strands of cotton over two threads of linen. Where two colours of thread are stipulated, thread a single strand of each colour together in the needle.

2 Work the back stitch using a single strand of linen. Count the threads carefully to find the correct position of the border.

3 Press on the reverse side with a damp cloth when complete.

TO MAKE UP

1 Tack a line 3½in (9cm) out from the stitched border. Cut an 18in (46cm) square from the canvas and draw out several 2½in (6cm) bias strips on the remaining piece (see page 30). Cut sufficient strips of bias to fit round the edge of the cushion.

2 Join the bias strips together and press the seams flat. Fold the bias strip over the piping cord and tack to hold the piping cord in place.

3 Beginning along the bottom edge of the cushion, pin and tack the piping along the tacked line on the right side with the raw edges facing out. Mark where the piping overlaps with pins, open out and join as before. Trim the excess cord and tack in place.

4 Using a zipper foot on the sewing machine, stitch close to the piping along the bottom edge only. With right sides together, pin and tack the berry canvas to the linen. Machine stitch along the remaining three sides.

5 Trim the seams and trim across the corners and turn through. Give the cushion cover a final press before inserting the cushion pad. Slip stitch the remaining side to finish.

SALT BOX

*M*ANY *companies produce bare 'blank' articles ready to paint and decorate. Look for a shape which can take an Aida band and stitch this delightful design adapted from a nineteenth-century border stencil.*

MATERIALS

- ❖ 24in (61cm) of 3½in (9cm) wide white woven-edge Aida band, Zweigart E7316, 44 stitches
- ❖ salt box blank
- ❖ tape measure
- ❖ pins
- ❖ DMC stranded cotton 347, 518, 814, 991, 993, 3328, 3765
- ❖ size 24 tapestry needle
- ❖ sandpaper
- ❖ blue-green reproduction paint, Colourman 136
- ❖ paint brush
- ❖ double-sided tape

TO STITCH

1 Measure round the front three sides of the salt box and mark this length centrally on the Aida band with pins. Fold the band in half crossways and begin stitching in the centre using two strands of cotton.

2 Work the repeats on either side of the centre panel out as far as the pin markers.

3 Turn under ½in (12mm) at each end and press on the reverse side.

TO MAKE UP

1 Sand the salt box blank lightly and paint.

2 Position the Aida band round the salt box and stick the ends down on the back of the box with double-sided tape.

DMC stranded cotton

CROSS STITCH KEY
- ■ DMC 814
- ■ DMC 3328
- ■ DMC 347
- ■ DMC 3765
- ■ DMC 991
- ■ DMC 993
- ■ DMC 518

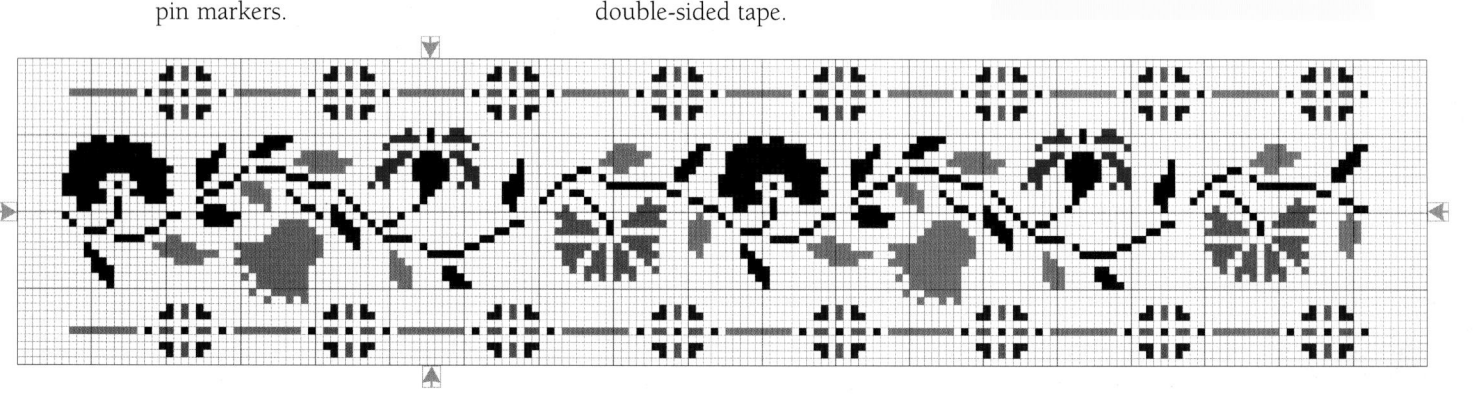

LEAFY TABLE MAT

*T*HIS *attractive white on blue leaf design is from an early American wallpaper pattern. Wallpaper was introduced in the late nineteenth century to take the place of stencilling as the New Englanders became a little more affluent.*

MATERIALS

- 14 x 17in (36 x 43cm) 32-count antique blue Belfast linen, Zweigart E3609
- scissors
- tacking thread
- needle
- tape measure
- Anchor Nordin flower thread 1
- size 26 tapestry needle
- tailor's wax (optional)
- sewing thread
- ½ yd (½m) of 36in (90cm) wide gingham fabric

TO STITCH

1 Tack a guideline across the linen 2in (5cm) from the edge. Fold the linen in half lengthways to find the centre point and work the cross stitch using a single thickness of flower thread over two threads of linen. You may find it easier to run the flower thread through the tailor's wax before stitching.

2 Work the back stitch then stitch a repeat on either side of the centre motif.

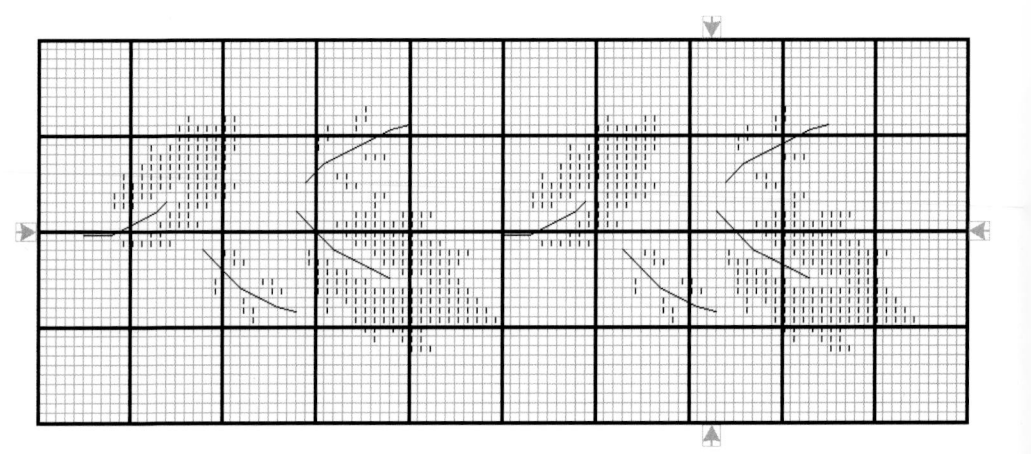

3 Press on the reverse side with a damp cloth.

TO MAKE UP

1 Cut a piece of gingham the same size as the linen, then pin and tack to the reverse side.

2 Cut and join sufficient 1in (5cm) wide bias strips in gingham to fit round the edge of the mat. To fit the binding round the corners, fold it up at right angles and then back on itself down the next side. Keep the fold along the top edge. Repeat on all four corners and

join the bias in the middle of one long side.

3 Stitch each side of the binding separately, taking care the flaps don't get caught in the stitching. Complete the binding as shown on page 31, mitring the corners neatly on both sides.

Anchor Nordin flower thread

CROSS STITCH KEY
I Anchor 1

BACKSTITCH KEY
= Anchor 1

COCKEREL CUSHION

*T*HRIFTY *and innovative, the early pioneers collected strips of old wool fabric to make warm and comfortable rugs. This charming cockerel design, worked in tapestry wool, has been adapted from a hooked rug made in 1893.*

MATERIALS

- ❖ 14in (36cm) square of 7-count interlocking canvas, Anchor FSL075
- ❖ Appleton tapestry wool, one skein of 964 and 972, two of 932, three of 989, four of 748
- ❖ size 16 tapestry needle
- ❖ plywood board or pinboard
- ❖ large map pins
- ❖ 18 x 36in (46 x 91cm) heavy-weight cream fabric
- ❖ tacking thread
- ❖ needle
- ❖ sewing thread
- ❖ 16in (40cm) cushion pad
- ❖ 1 yd (91cm) navy cord
- ❖ 4 small cream tassels

TO STITCH

1 Fold the canvas in four to find the centre point and work the cross stitch using a single thickness of tapestry wool. Use at most a 20in (50cm) length of wool as a longer length may begin to thin towards the end and give poor coverage of the canvas. The canvas can be stitched with or without a frame. Unlike needlepoint which tends to pull the canvas diagonally, cross stitched canvas remains square.

2 Once the design is complete, it needs to be 'blocked' to even out the stitches and remove any creases from the canvas. To do this, follow the detailed instructions on page 28. Pin the canvas on top of the board, stretching it slightly as you go. Spray the cross stitch lightly with water until it is slightly damp and allow to dry away from direct heat.

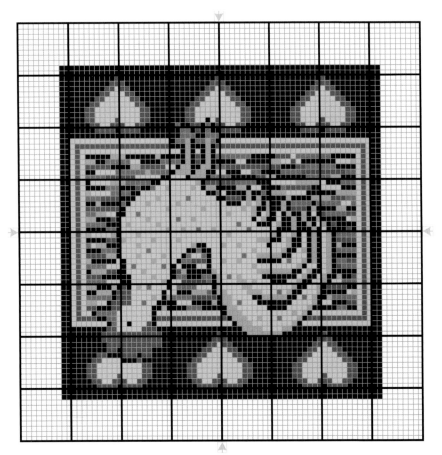

TO MAKE UP

1 Cut the cream fabric in half crossways. Trim the canvas, leaving ½in (12 mm) seam allowance round the edge. Turn the seam allowance to the reverse side and pin the cross stitch panel to the centre of one square of fabric. Tack lines across the middle as well as round the edge to prevent the panel creeping while it is slip stitched neatly in position.

2 With right sides together, pin and tack round the edge of the cushion. Machine stitch 1in (2.5cm) from the raw edge, leaving a large gap along the bottom. Trim across the corners and turn through.

3 Insert the cushion pad and slip stitch across the gap. Snip a few stitches at each corner of the cushion and insert the tassel cords. Sew the tassels securely to each corner.

Appleton tapestry wool

CROSS STITCH KEY

Appleton 972
Appleton 989
Appleton 932
Appleton 748
Appleton 964

FLOWER POT PICTURE

*T*HE *unusual border design round this delightful pot of flowers is made up of tiny areas of different coloured embroidery threads. This is a similar style to the hooked rugs made by resourceful pioneers from their collections of multi-coloured scraps of wool.*

MATERIALS

❖ 16in (40cm) square of 27-count black Linda evenweave, Zweigart E1235

❖ tacking thread

❖ Anchor Nordin flower thread 8, 10, 22, 54, 120, 147, 185, 188, 288, 292, 922

❖ size 24 tapestry needle

❖ tailor's wax (optional)

❖ scissors

❖ mountboard

❖ pencil ruler

❖ strong thread

❖ picture frame

Anchor Nordin flower thread

CROSS STITCH KEY

■ Anchor 922
■ Anchor 22
■ Anchor 188
■ Anchor 147
□ Anchor 292
■ Anchor 8
■ Anchor 10
□ Anchor 288
■ Anchor 185
■ Anchor 54
■ Anchor 120

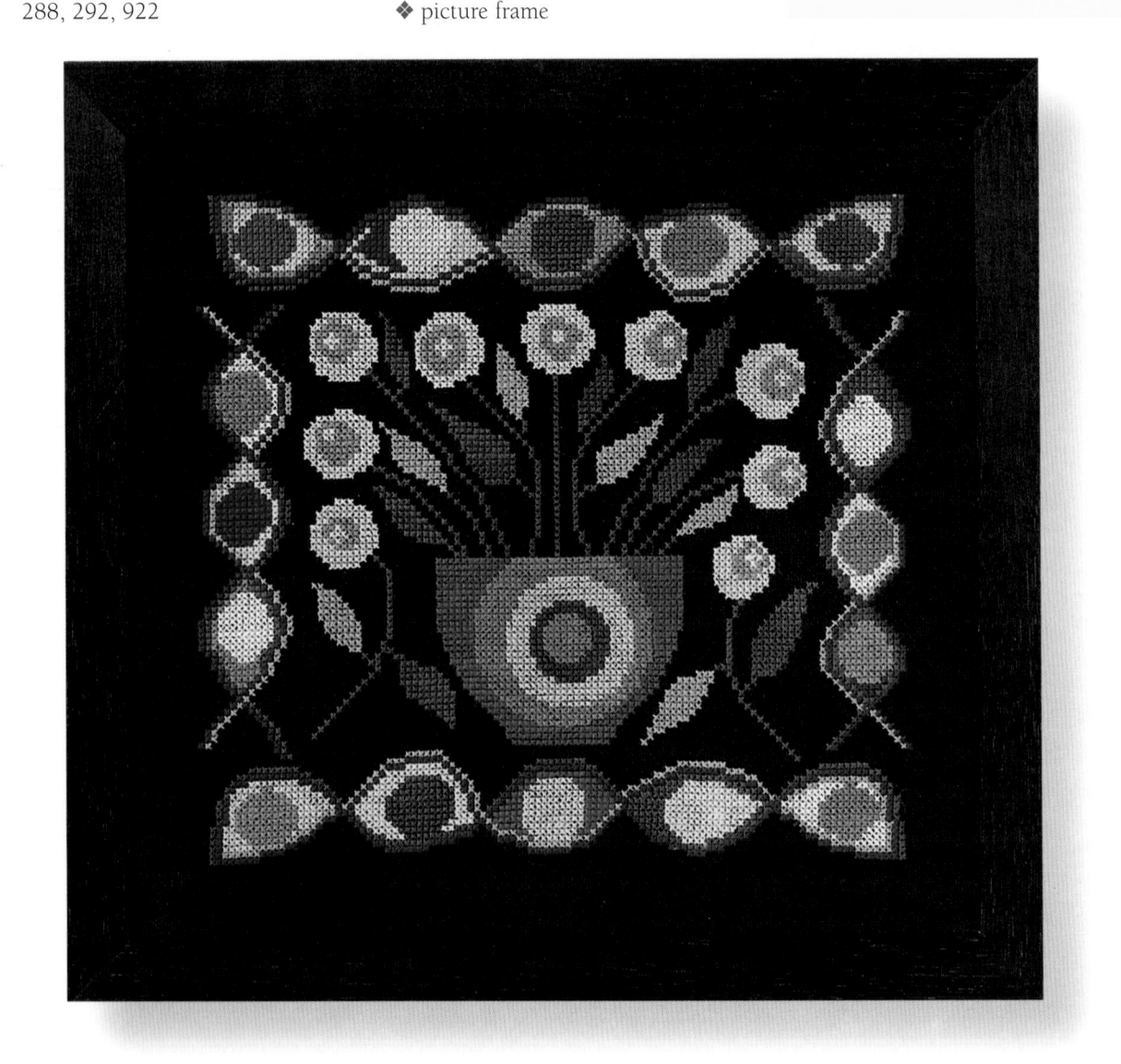

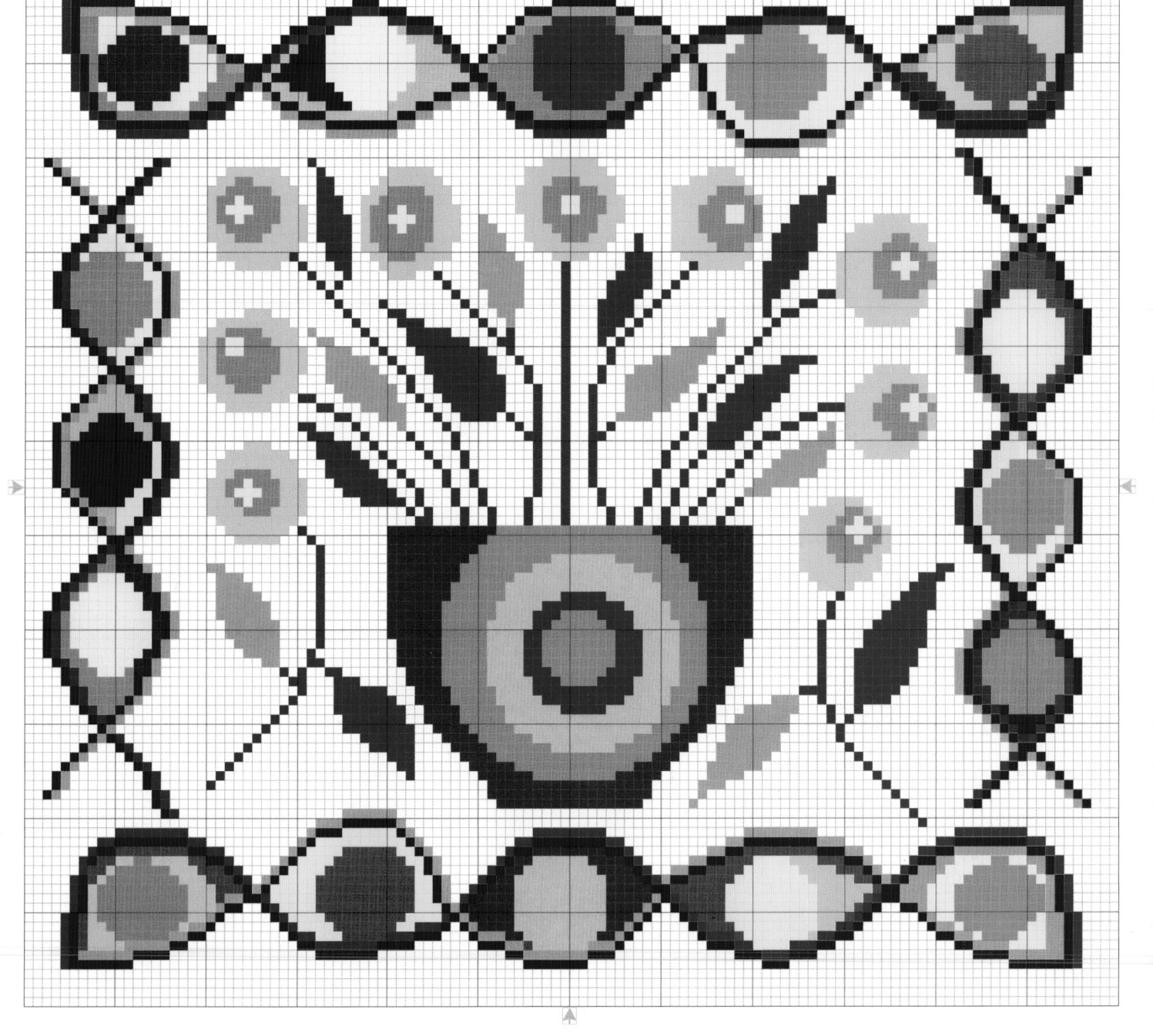

TO STITCH

1 Tack guidelines in both directions across the centre of the linen. Work the cross stitch using a single thickness of flower thread. You may find it easier to run the flower thread through the tailor's wax before stitching.

2 Press the design on the reverse side when complete.

TO MAKE UP

1 Measure the mountboard and mark the centre point on each side. Lay the embroidery face down on a flat surface and position the mount-board on top, matching the centre marks to the tacked guidelines.

2 Stretch the evenweave over the mountboard as shown on page 33 and fit in a frame of your choice.

LINEN TIE-BACKS

THE contrasting patterns in this rustic design emulate traditional star quilt blocks which generally show symmetrical stars with an even number of points so that they can be easily made out of triangles or diamonds.

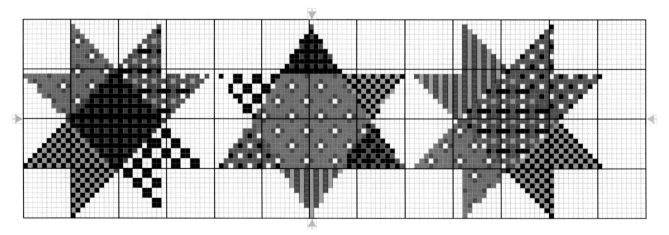

MATERIALS

Makes two 12in (30cm) tie-backs

❖ 3 yds (2.75 m) of 4¾in (12cm) wide scalloped-edge raw linen band, Zweigart E7273, 41 stitches
❖ scissors
❖ Anchor Nordin flower thread 150, 372, 373, 903, 926, 9046
❖ size 24 tapestry needle
❖ tacking thread
❖ needle
❖ pins
❖ four 1in (2.5cm) brass curtain rings

TO STITCH

1 Cut the linen band in four and put two pieces aside for the second tie-back. Fold one piece in half cross-ways to find the centre. Work the left-hand star motif in the centre of the linen band using a single thickness of flower thread over two threads of linen. Work the other two star motifs on the right-hand side and press with a damp cloth on the reverse side when complete.

2 Work the second tie-back in a mirror image with the star motifs on the left-hand side.

CROSS STITCH KEY

Anchor Nordin flower thread

☐ Anchor 926
▨ Anchor 9046
■ Anchor 150
▨ Anchor 373
▨ Anchor 903
▨ Anchor 372

TO MAKE UP

1 Lay the embroidered band face down on a flat surface. Fold over ½in (12mm) at each end and then bring the corners into the centre to make a triangular point. Fold the other end in the same way and press with a damp cloth.

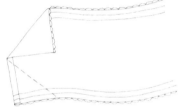

2 Turn in the ends of the lining piece in the same way. With the reverse sides together, pin and tack the two bands together. Stitch the two bands together along the woven decorative edge with red running stitch.

3 Insert a brass ring between the layers of linen at the end of the band. Stitch a row of running stitch ¼in (5 mm) from the edge, catching in the ring as you go.

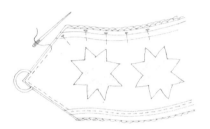

The same cross stitch design can be used to make a larger 15in (38cm) tie-back. You will need 3½ yds (3.2 m) of linen cut in four. Stitch all three star motifs to one side of the centre line and complete as above.

Complete the second tie-back in the same way.

CONTEMPORARY DESIGNS

❖

American folk art has never been more popular and this has a great deal to do with the increasing appreciation for country style. The simple appeal of folk art fits well with the natural furnishings and homespun fabric used in homes today. Inspired by traditional folk art, these cross stitch designs have been developed using contemporary colours and ideas. Stitch a pretty herb or spice hanging for the kitchen, the delightful leaping hares on a cushion or you could choose the pencil pot or egg cabinet featuring the stars and stripes.

THE PROJECTS

Flag pencil pot
Stars and stripes apron
Herb-filled hearts
Mini-cushion hanging
Apple notebook cover
Poinsettia tote bag
Patchwork mirror frame
Watermelon napkin
Egg cabinet
Spiced hot pad
Watermelon picture
Leaping hare cushion

FLAG PENCIL POT

*T*HROUGHOUT *America has experienced great periods of patriotism and the favourite symbol for folk artists is the American flag. Here the flag has been enclosed in the quintessential five pointed star.*

MATERIALS

- ❖ 4in (10cm) square of red stitch-ing paper, Inglestone Collection
- ❖ Anchor stranded cotton 1, 44, 47, 127, 146
- ❖ size 24 tapestry needle
- ❖ scissors
- ❖ blank pencil pot
- ❖ red and off-white reproduction paint, Colourman 107, 116
- ❖ paint brush
- ❖ sandpaper
- ❖ pencil
- ❖ double-sided tape

TO STITCH

1 Stitching paper is very easy to use and ideal for a small project like this because it doesn't fray. Care must be taken, however, when stitching so that the paper doesn't tear. If necessary it can be repaired with sticky tape and the holes repunched using a large needle.

2 Stitch the design using two strands of cotton, taking the needle up and down in a stabbing action to prevent any tears. Trim the stitch-ing paper close to the cross stitch, taking care not to snip any stitches.

TO MAKE UP

1 Paint the pencil pot with two thin coats of red paint and allow to dry.

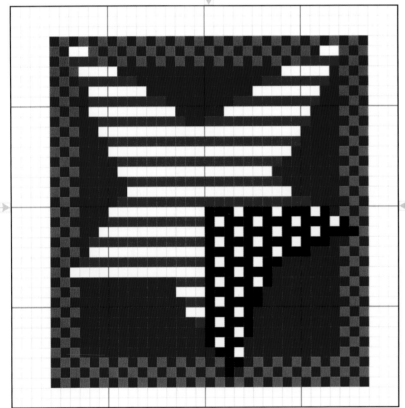

Paint over the red on the outside with two coats of off-white paint. Once the paint is dry, rub down the edges to reveal a little red paint.

2 Hold the cross stitch panel in posi-tion on one side of the pot and mark a dot with a pencil at each corner.

3 Stick double-sided tape all over the back of the cross stitch panel. Remove the backing paper and carefully stick in position inside the pencil marks.

Anchor stranded cotton

CROSS STITCH KEY

□ Anchor 1
▨ Anchor 146
▤ Anchor 47
▦ Anchor 44
■ Anchor 127

STARS AND STRIPES
APRON

*E*VER *since the star spangled banner first flew in Baltimore in 1812, the American people have had a love affair with stars and stripes. Here the archetypal five-pointed stars are stitched on an attractive navy and white striped apron.*

MATERIALS

❖ large navy and white striped bib apron

❖ 8in (20cm) square of 10-count waste canvas

❖ pins

❖ tacking thread

❖ needle

❖ Anchor Nordin flower thread 9046

❖ size 24 tapestry needle

❖ tailor's wax (optional)

❖ scissors

TO STITCH

1 Pin and tack the waste canvas in the middle of the bib, 2in (5cm) down from the top edge. Begin the cross stitch border 3in (8cm) down from the top edge.

2 Work the cross stitches as evenly as possible using a single thickness of flower thread. You may find it easier to stitch the flower thread through the apron if each length is lightly waxed before stitching.

3 Once the cross stitch is complete, remove the tacking thread and begin to fray the canvas. Remove all the threads running parallel to the outside border and then begin to take out the rest. Pull out the canvas threads carefully one at a time using a pair of tweezers for grip if required.

4 Press on the reverse side with a damp cloth.

Anchor Nordin flower thread

CROSS STITCH KEY
■ Anchor 9046

HERB-FILLED HEARTS

*IF folk art is something which is both functional and decorative,
these sweet smelling little heart pillows, strung together on red
ribbon, are the perfect example and would make a
delightful gift for a friend.*

MATERIALS

❖ 9in (23cm) square of 28-count
antique white Cashel linen,
Zweigart E3281
❖ Anchor Nordin flower thread 47,
134
❖ size 24 tapestry needle
❖ tailor's wax (optional)
❖ 8in (20cm) of 36in (90cm) wide
red, white and blue check fabric
❖ scissors
❖ pencil
❖ tracing paper
❖ sewing thread
❖ needle
❖ polyester stuffing
❖ fresh herbs in a muslin sachet
❖ 18in (46cm) of ¼in (7 mm) wide
ribbon
❖ two ⅝in (1.5cm) red four-hole
buttons

TO STITCH

1 Work the cross stitch in the middle
of the linen using a single thickness of flower thread over two
threads of linen. You may find it
easier to stitch the flower thread if
each length is lightly waxed before
stitching.

2 Press on the reverse side with a
damp cloth when complete.

TO MAKE UP

1 Cut an 8in (20cm) square of check
fabric. With right sides together,
pin to the cross stitched linen. Tack
a heart shape ⅕in (5 mm) round
the outside of the cross stitch.

2 Stitch on the outside of
the tacking leaving a 2in
(5cm) gap along one straight
side. Trim the seams and notch the
curves before turning through.
Ease out the point and press.

3 Cut four 6in (15cm) squares of
check fabric. Trace and cut out the
heart template. Pin on top of the
squares and cut out four hearts.

4 With right sides together, pin and tack two hearts together. Stitch ¼in (5 mm) from the edge, leaving a gap on a straight side as before. Stitch the other two heart pieces together. Trim the seams and notch the curves before turning through. Ease out the points and press.

5 Fill each of the hearts with polyester stuffing. Push the stuffing into the point and curves with the end of a pencil. Push the muslin sachet into the large cushion and slip stitch the gaps to complete.

6 Cut the ribbon into three equal pieces. Fold the pieces in half to form loops and stitch securely to the top of each heart. Using blue flower thread, sew a button on to the bottom of the linen heart and one of the small hearts. Arrange the hearts with the linen heart in the middle and fasten the top of the loop to the button of the next heart. Hang the hearts from the top ribbon loop.

Anchor Nordin flower thread

CROSS STITCH KEY
■ Anchor 134
■ Anchor 47

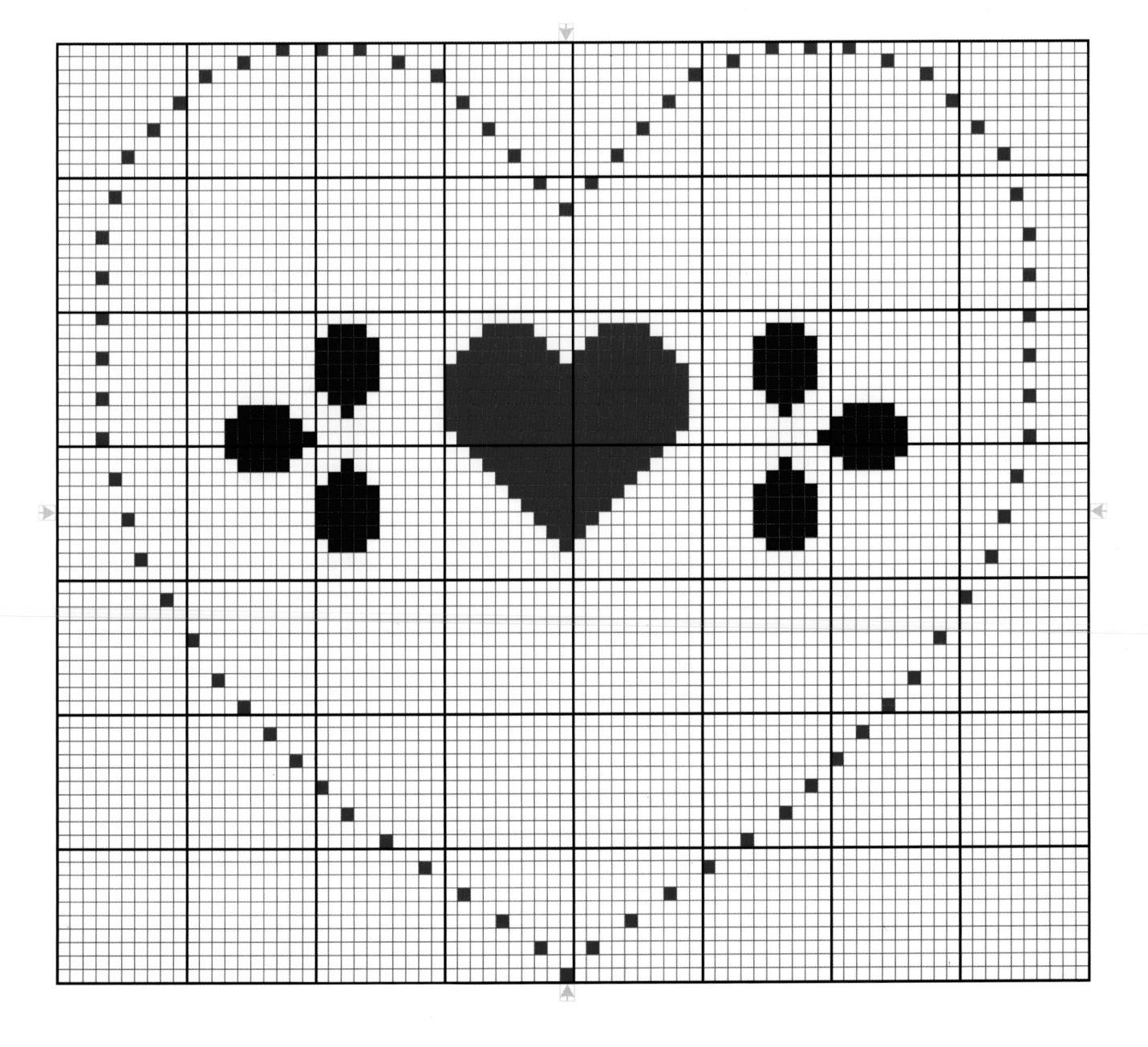

MINI-CUSHION HANGING

A delightful decoration combining the classic folk art themes of hearts and gingham, this little cushion can be filled with cinnamon sticks or other spices which will produce a wonderful aroma in a warm kitchen.

MATERIALS

- ❖ two 9in (23cm) squares of 30-count antique blue linen, Zweigart E3609
- ❖ Anchor Nordin flower thread 47, 134, 275
- ❖ size 24 tapestry needle
- ❖ tailor's wax (optional)
- ❖ tacking thread
- ❖ needle
- ❖ 20in (50cm) of ⅝in (1.5cm) red gingham ribbon
- ❖ scissors
- ❖ pins
- ❖ sewing thread
- ❖ two 7in (18cm) squares of white cotton
- ❖ polyester stuffing

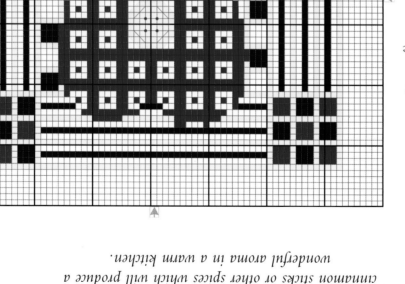

Anchor Nordin flower thread

CROSS STITCH KEY
□ Anchor 275
■ Anchor 47
■ Anchor 134

BACK STITCH KEY
— Anchor 134

FRENCH KNOT KEY
:: Anchor 47

TO STITCH

1. Fold the linen in four to find the centre and work the cross stitch using a single thickness of flower thread over two threads of linen. You may find it easier to stitch the flower thread if each length is lightly waxed wax before use.

2. Press on the reverse side with a damp cloth when complete.

TO MAKE UP

1. Tack a 6in (15cm) square guide line round the cross stitch, positioning the cross stitch just above the centre. Cut the ribbon in half. Pin and tack one end of each piece of ribbon over the tacking line close to the edge of the embroidered panel.

2. Wrap the long ends into a bundle in the middle of the cross stitch panel. Lay the second piece of

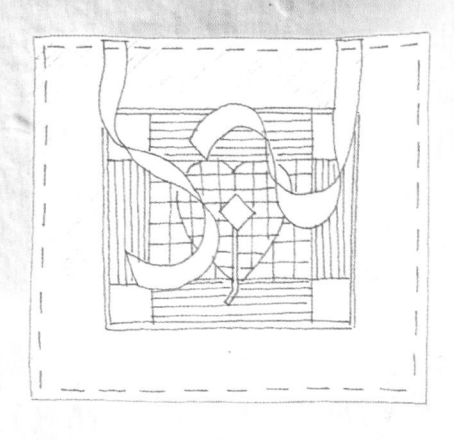

linen on top. Pin the two layers together and stitch along the previous tacking line leaving a 4in (10cm) gap along the bottom.

3 Trim the seams and trim across the corners then turn through. Ease out the corners and press on the reverse side with a damp cloth.

4 To make the cushion pad, stitch the two pieces of white cotton together leaving a gap on one side. Trim across the corners and turn through. Fill the cushion pad with stuffing, using a pencil to get it right into the corners. Tack the gap and machine stitch.

5 Insert the pad into the mini cushion and slip stitch the gap. Tie the ends of the ribbon into a bow and trim the ends diagonally ready to hang the cushion.

APPLE NOTEBOOK COVER

*T*HE *phrase 'as American as apple pie' inspired the choice of motif for the front of this recipe book. The rosy red apple motif stitched on white linen is the ideal reminder that this book contains all your favourite recipes.*

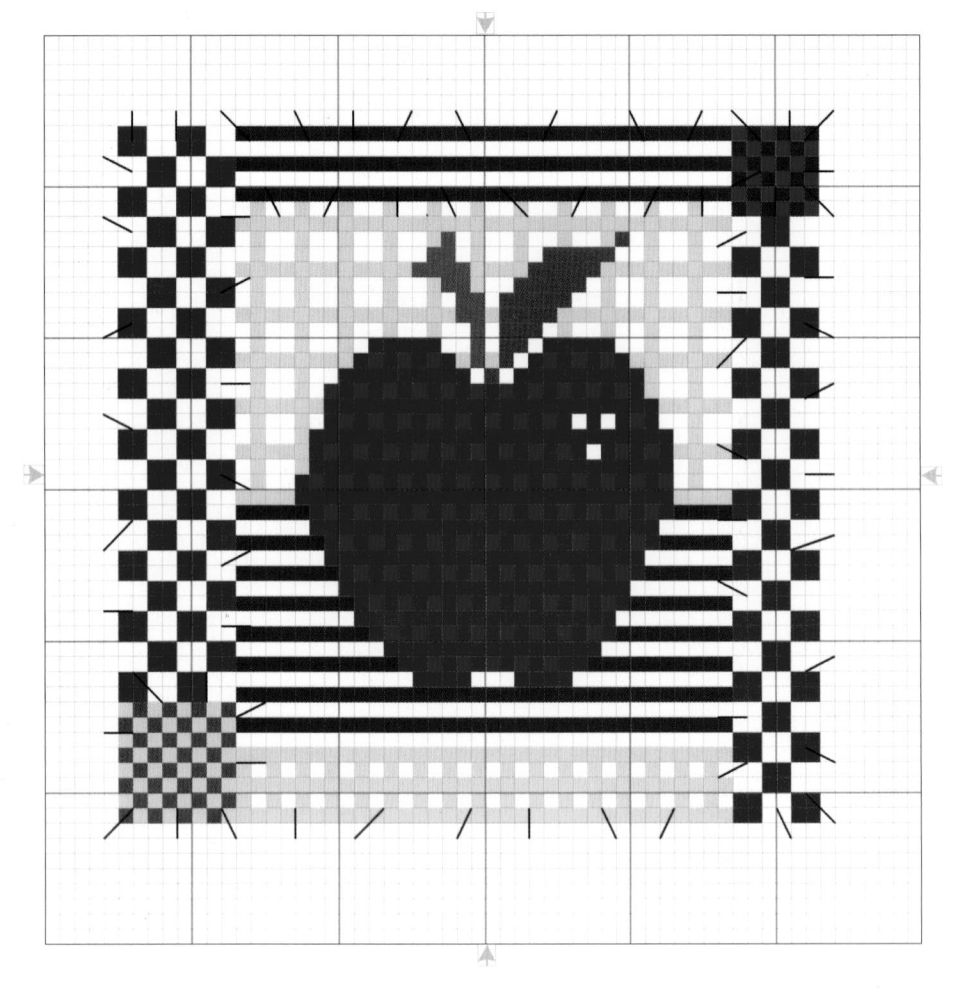

MATERIALS

- 8in (20cm) square of 28-count antique white Cashel linen, E3281
- DMC stranded cotton 312, 321, 336, 676, 815, 840, 3808
- size 24 tapestry needle
- 14 x 18in (36 x 46cm) navy and white ticking
- 6in (15cm) square of fusible bonding web

- 6in (15cm) square of yellow gingham
- pinking shears
- pins
- tacking thread
- scissors
- 8 x 12in (20 x 30cm) iron-on wadding
- A5 notebook

DMC stranded cotton

CROSS STITCH KEY
- ■ DMC 840
- ■ DMC 676
- ■ DMC 312
- ■ DMC 815
- ■ DMC 321
- ■ DMC 3808

BACK STITCH KEY
- ═ DMC 336

TO STITCH

1 Fold the linen in quarters to find the centre. Work the cross stitch design in the middle of the linen using two strands of cotton over two threads of linen. Don't stitch any of the back stitch at this stage.

2 Press the linen on the reverse side with a damp cloth.

TO MAKE UP

1 Iron the fusible bonding web on to the reverse side of the yellow gingham. Carefully cut out a 4¾in (12cm) square with pinking shears and remove the backing paper.

2 Tuck the notebook inside the navy and white ticking. Pin and tack the yellow gingham just above the centre of the front cover. Iron the gingham in position.

3 Trim the embroidered panel ½in (12 mm) from the cross stitch. Turn the seam allowance to the reverse side, mitre the corners neatly (see page 30) and press in position.

4 Tack the cross stitch panel in the centre of the yellow gingham. Work the back stitch through all the layers of fabric, following the chart. Take out any remaining tacking thread.

5 Cut the iron-on wadding in two crossways and iron on to the front and back covers of the book.

6 Follow the instructions on page 41 to finish covering the book.

POINSETTIA TOTE BAG

WITH its bright red bracts and deep green leaves, the poinsettia has become a popular motif at Christmas time. This delightful little bag is large enough for a small gift or could be hung on the tree.

MATERIALS

- ❖ 12 x 24in (30 x 61cm) 30-count evergreen Belfast linen, Zweigart E3609
- ❖ tape measure
- ❖ scissors
- ❖ Anchor stranded cotton 22, 46, 47, 217, 218, 293, 295, 926
- ❖ size 26 tapestry needle
- ❖ 7 x 10in (18 x 25cm) red silk
- ❖ pins
- ❖ sewing thread
- ❖ needle
- ❖ bodkin or safety pin
- ❖ tacking thread

TO STITCH

1 Cut a 4 x 10in (10 x 25cm) strip of linen for the straps and set aside. Fold the remaining piece in four to mark the centre lines. Measure 2¾in (7cm) up from the crossways fold line and mark the centre point of the design.

2 Work the cross stitch using a single strand of cotton over two threads of linen. Once complete, work the back stitch. Fill the centre area with French knots stitched using two strands of cotton.

3 Press on the reverse side with a damp cloth.

TO MAKE UP

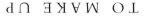

1 Trim ⅜in (9mm) from the cross stitched linen along the straight grain to make a 7 x 13¾in (18 x 34cm) strip. Fold over ¼in (5mm) to the reverse side on each short side and machine stitch.

2 With right sides together, fold the linen in half crossways and stitch the side seams. Fold the bottom corners up until the folded edge

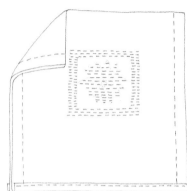

touches the side of the embroidered panel. Crease with your finger to mark the bias line and stitch. Trim the seams and turn them through.

3 Fold the silk in half crossways and stitch the side seams and bias corners to match the linen bag. Press the silk lining and tuck it inside the linen bag, wrong sides together, matching the side seams. Turn down the top edge of the linen to make a 1in (2.5cm) hem on the inside. Tuck the silk underneath and pin.

7 Press on the reverse side with a damp cloth.

Anchor stranded cotton

CROSS STITCH KEY
☐ Anchor 926
▨ Anchor 293
■ Anchor 46
■ Anchor 47
■ Anchor 217

BACK STITCH KEY
— Anchor 22
— Anchor 218

FRENCH KNOT KEY
⠿ Anchor 295

6 Repeat with the back strap, lining it up behind the front strap, and tack right round the bag. Machine stitch ¾in (2cm) down from the fold line and again ¼in (5mm) from the fold to secure the straps and the lining.

5 Press the ends of the straps over ¾in (2cm) to the right side and tuck under the inside hem on the front of the bag. Line up the strap with both sides of the cross stitched panel and tack securely.

4 To make the straps, cut the set aside linen strip in two length-ways. Fold the strips in half and machine ¼in (5mm) from the raw edge. Press the seam open, turn the strips through using a bodkin or safety pin and press with the seam down the centre back.

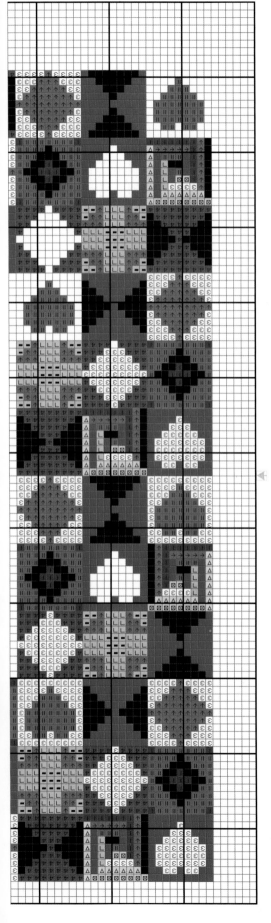

PATCHWORK MIRROR FRAME

CONTEMPORARY artists making pieced quilts have ensured that patchwork has reached the status of modern folk art. This particularly charming cross stitch design brings together some traditional blocks in a thoroughly modern way. The pattern is based on a nine-square block which is repeated round the frame, working it inverted or flipped to make to make a balanced design.

MATERIALS

- ❖ 14in (36cm) square of 25-count white evenweave, Anchor FSE25M
- ❖ DMC stranded cotton 1, 336, 347, 666, 3760
- ❖ 9in (23cm) square of mountboard
- ❖ 9 x 18in (23 x 46cm) foam core
- ❖ double-sided tape
- ❖ 5in (13cm) mirror tile
- ❖ craft knife
- ❖ safety ruler
- ❖ cutting mat
- ❖ scissors
- ❖ pencil
- ❖ white gummed tape
- ❖ two stick-on picture hangers

TO STITCH

1 Work the cross stitch design beginning in one corner 3in (7.5cm) from the edge of the linen. Use two strands of cotton over two threads of linen.

2 Where two colours are stipulated, thread a single strand of each colour together in the needle.

3 Press on the reverse side with a damp cloth when complete.

TO MAKE UP

1 Cut the mountboard to the exact size of the cross stitch design. Measure the width of the border and transfer to the mountboard. Cut out the centre panel – approximately a 4¼in (11cm) square.

2 Cut a square of foam core the same size as the mountboard. Cut four 1½in (4cm) strips of foam core and trim to fit round the edge of the square. Stick the pieces in position with double-sided tape and stick the mirror tile in the middle.

3 Lay the cross stitch panel face down on a flat surface. Snip into the middle of the centre area and carefully cut diagonally out to each corner. Trim across the triangle flaps to leave 1in (2.5cm) seam allowance.

DMC stranded cotton

CROSS STITCH KEY
⌐ DMC 336+1
■ DMC 336
▮ DMC 336+666
‖ DMC 666
3 DMC 1
⬥ DMC 347
▪ DMC 3760
↓ DMC 336+3760
← DMC 666+3760
▽ DMC 666+1
■ DMC 347+1
⊠ DMC 3760+1

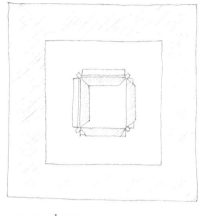

4 Stick double-sided tape round the inner edge of the mountboard frame. Stick an extra little piece on the cut edge of each corner. Lay the mountboard frame on top of the cross stitch. Stretch the linen flaps on to the double-sided tape, keeping the edge of the cross stitch straight. Press down firmly, making sure any tiny snipped threads in the corners are stuck down.

5 Stick double-sided tape round the outside cut edge of the foam core frame. Stick a few pieces of double-sided tape on the front of the foam core and remove the backing paper. Position the covered mountboard over the foam core and stick together. Remove the backing paper from the rest of the double-sided tape and gently stretch the linen. Stick the linen down completely along the top and bottom edges of the frame. Fold the excess fabric in at the side and stick down neatly.

6 Fold the linen under on the reverse side. Cover any raw edges with white gummed tape. Stick two picture hangers on the back near the top edge to hang.

WATERMELON NAPKIN

MATERIALS

❖ 18in (46cm) square of sage green Quaker cloth for each napkin, Zweigart E3993

❖ tacking thread

❖ needle

❖ tape measure

❖ Anchor Nordin flower thread 59, 218, 275, 403

❖ size 24 tapestry needle

❖ tailor's wax (optional)

❖ sewing thread

❖ scissors

*W*ITH *its bold colours and appealing curved shape, the watermelon has become one of the most popular folk art motifs today. This simple motif is quick to sew and the napkin makes an ideal accessory for a picnic on a hot and humid summer day.*

TO STITCH

1 Tack guidelines in the bottom left hand corner of the evenweave, 4in (10cm) in from the edge. Count up 38 threads from the guideline and begin to stitch the motif, working a single thickness of flower thread over two threads of evenweave. You may find it easier to stitch flower thread through linen if each length is lightly waxed before use.

2 Tack a further guideline 1½in (4cm) in from the edge of the fabric. Beginning in the centre of each side, work large green cross stitches outside the tacking line. Sew each cross stitch over eight threads leaving a space of eight threads between the stitches. Work red, cream and black cross stitches over four threads in the middle of the spaces round the edge of the napkin.

TO MAKE UP

1 Turn under the edge of the napkin four threads from the stitching and press. Trim the hem allowance to 1in (2.5cm). Turn under a ⅝in (1.5cm) hem, mitre the corners (see page 30) and slip stitch in position. Work a red French knot in each corner.

2 Press on the reverse side with a damp cloth to complete.

Anchor Nordin flower thread

CROSS STITCH KEY
■ Anchor 403
■ Anchor 218
③ Anchor 275
▦ Anchor 59

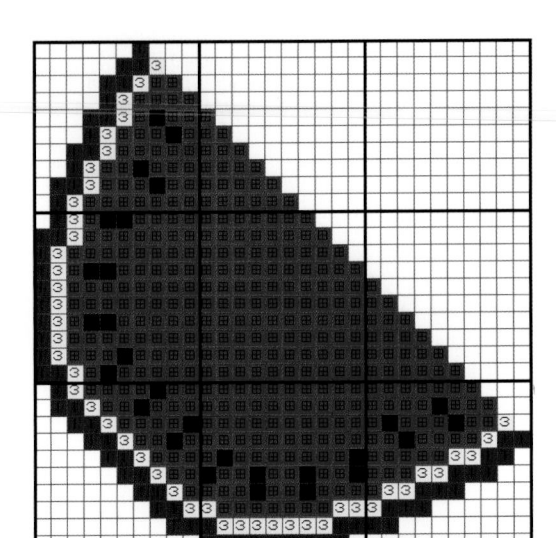

EGG CABINET

ONE of the most useful items to have in a country kitchen is an egg cabinet. The eggs keep better at room temperature and are ready for use in baking straight away. This patriotic design leaves no doubt about what's inside.

MATERIALS

- ❖ 10in (25cm) square of 28-count natural Quaker cloth, Zweigart E3993
- ❖ tacking thread
- ❖ needle
- ❖ Anchor Nordin flower thread 2, 13, 134
- ❖ tailor's wax (optional)
- ❖ 8in (20cm) square of mountboard
- ❖ craft knife
- ❖ safety ruler
- ❖ strong thread
- ❖ cutting mat
- ❖ egg cabinet
- ❖ red reproduction paint, Colourman 116
- ❖ paint brush
- ❖ sand paper
- ❖ clear beeswax
- ❖ 8in (20cm) square of hardboard
- ❖ panel pins
- ❖ hammer

TO STITCH

1 Tack a guideline across the evenweave in both directions to mark the centre lines. Work the cross stitch using a single thickness of flower thread over two threads of evenweave. You may find it easier to run the flower thread through the evenweave before stitching. Work the back stitch.

2 Press on the reverse side with a damp cloth when complete.

TO MAKE UP

1 Measure the door recess, cut the mountboard to fit and mark the centre point on each side. Lay the embroidery face down on a flat surface and position the mountboard on top, matching the centre marks to the tacked guidelines. Stretch the evenweave over the mountboard as shown on page 33.

2 The door of the egg cabinet must have a recess like a picture frame and may need to be routed by a carpenter. Paint the egg cabinet with two thin coats of paint and allow to dry. Rub down the edges of the cabinet to distress the paint-work and apply a coat of beeswax to finish.

3 Insert the cross stitch into the recess in the door. Cut the hardboard to fit and fix in place with panel pins.

Anchor Nordin flower thread

CROSS STITCH KEY
□ Anchor 2
■ Anchor 134
▨ Anchor 13

BACK STITCH KEY
— Anchor 134

SPICED HOT PAD

SPRINKLE a few drops of spicy aromatherapy oil on this lovely mat. The scent will be released when a hot dish is placed on top. Decorated with a charming little gingerbread man, it not only looks good but protects your table top or work surface as well.

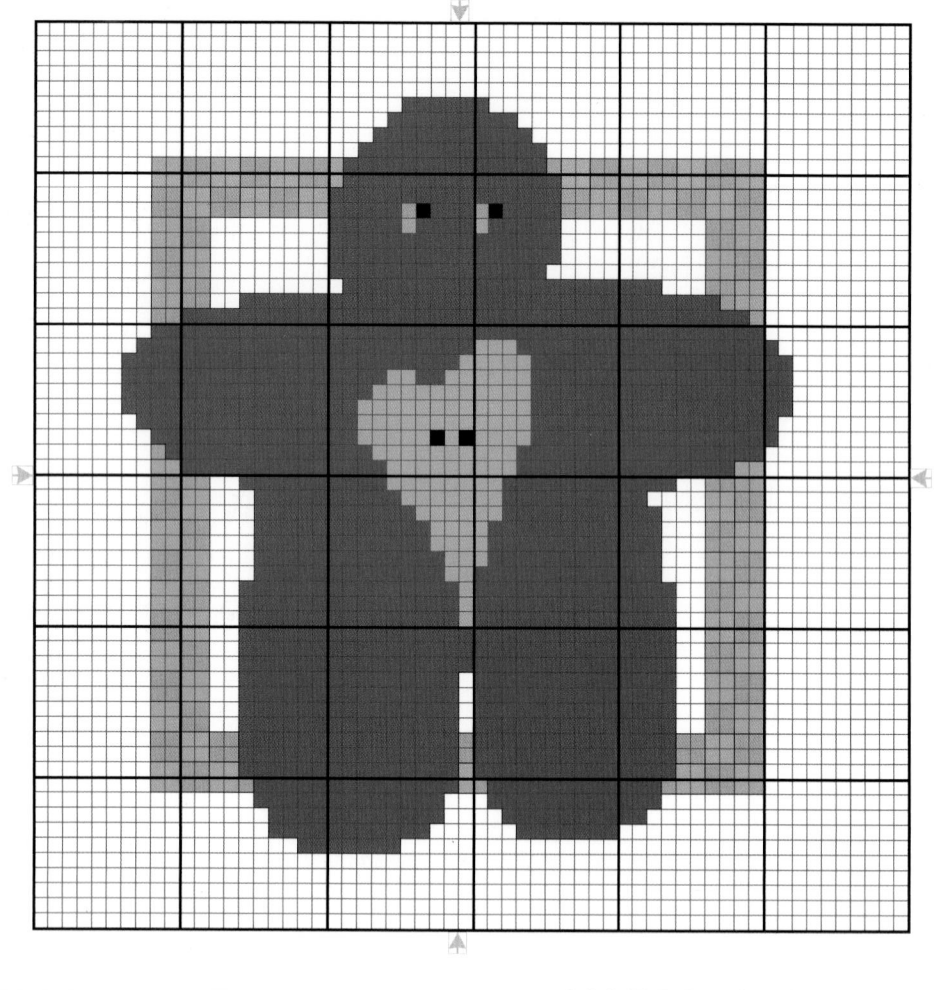

Anchor Nordin flower thread

CROSS STITCH KEY

■ Anchor 365
▨ Anchor 372
■ Anchor 127 (stranded cotton)
▥ Anchor 891

Anchor stranded cotton

BACKSTITCH KEY
═ Anchor 127

MATERIALS

- ❖ 10in (25cm) square of 28-count wine red Brittney evenweave, Zweigart E3270
- ❖ Anchor Nordin flower thread 365, 372, 891
- ❖ Anchor stranded cotton 127
- ❖ 10 x 22in (25 x 56cm) home-spun gingham
- ❖ size 24 tapestry needle
- ❖ scissors
- ❖ tape measure
- ❖ sewing thread
- ❖ 1⅛ yds (1m) size 2 piping cord
- ❖ 10in (25cm) square of 2oz (50g) wadding
- ❖ pins
- ❖ tacking thread
- ❖ needle
- ❖ pencil
- ❖ aromatherapy oil

TO STITCH

1 Fold the linen in four to find the centre point and work the cross stitch using a single thickness of flower thread. Stitch the button-holes and eye detail using two strands of dark blue.

2 Once all the cross stitch is complete, work the back stitch using a single strand of cotton.

3 Press the design on the reverse side with a damp cloth.

TO MAKE UP

1 Cut a 10in (25cm) square of gingham and set aside. Cut the remainder of the fabric into 1½in (4cm) wide bias strips (see page 30). Join the strips together, press the seams open and trim.

2 Fold the bias strips round the piping cord and tack (see page 31). Pin the piping in place, beginning in the middle of the bottom edge. Match the raw edges together and snip into the corners as required.

3 Open out the ends of the bias strip and mark where they overlap. Join the ends together as before, press the seam open and trim the piping cord to fit. Tack the piping in position and machine, using a zipper foot, along the bottom edge only.

4 With right sides together, pin and tack the gingham square to the linen. Machine close to the piping leaving a large gap along the bottom edge. Remove all the tacking thread.

5 Trim the seams and across the corners before turning through. Press the cover on the reverse side. Trim the wadding to fit inside and insert into the cover making sure it goes right into the corners.

6 Slip stitch the gap. To hold the wadding in place, stitch a yellow cross stitch in each corner through all the layers. Sprinkle a few drops of spicy aromatherapy oil on to the hot pad. A lovely smell will be released every time a hot dish is placed on the pad.

WATERMELON PICTURE

SUCH is the appeal of the watermelon as a folk art motif that it has featured in many different media like hooked rug designs, stencils and paintings. The subtle shading and intense colours in this cross stitch design have been achieved using blended threads and tones of green and red.

MATERIALS

- 15in (38cm) square of 28-count natural Quaker cloth, Zweigart E3993
- DMC stranded cotton 1, 310, 319, 320, 349, 350, 367, 369, 817, 824, 890
- size 24 tapestry needle
- tacking thread
- needle
- 8in (20cm) square of mountboard
- ruler
- pencil
- strong thread
- picture frame

TO STITCH

1 Tack guidelines across the centre of the evenweave in both directions. Work the cross stitch using two strands of cotton over two threads of linen. Where two colours are stipulated, thread a single strand of each colour together in the needle and sew as normal.

2 Work the back stitch using a single strand of cotton.

3 Press on the reverse side with a damp cloth.

DMC stranded cotton

CROSS STITCH KEY

- ◣ DMC 310
- ☐ DMC 1
- ▧ DMC 824
- ▨ DMC 824+1
- ⊥ DMC 349
- ▤ DMC 350
- ⊞ DMC 817
- ↓ DMC 350+349
- ▽ DMC 890
- ◙ DMC 319
- ◮ DMC 367
- ▬ DMC 320
- ☐ DMC 369
- ↑ DMC 350+320
- ◙ DMC 320+1

BACK STITCH KEY

- — DMC 320
- — DMC 319

TO MAKE UP

1 Measure the mountboard and mark the centre point on each side. Lay the embroidery face down on a flat surface and position the mountboard on top, matching the centre marks to the tacked guidelines.

2 Stretch the evenweave over the mountboard as shown on page 33 and fit in a frame of your choice.

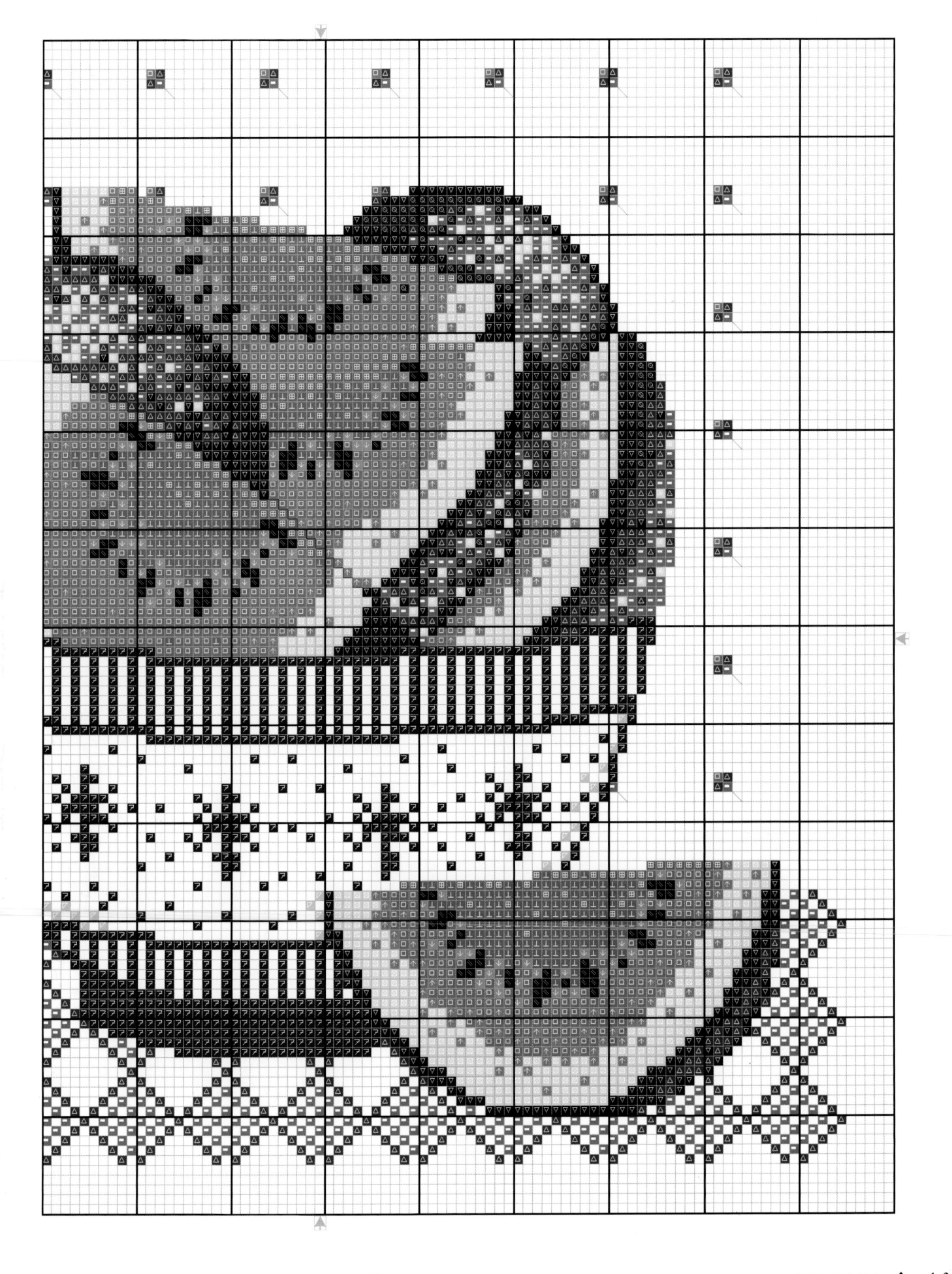

LEAPING HARE CUSHION

*C*HARMING *and whimsical animal motifs originally featured on early American hooked rugs. Hand-drawn primitive designs like this leaping hare are still as popular today. The earth tones in this cushion are reminiscent of the early natural dyes made from berries and bark.*

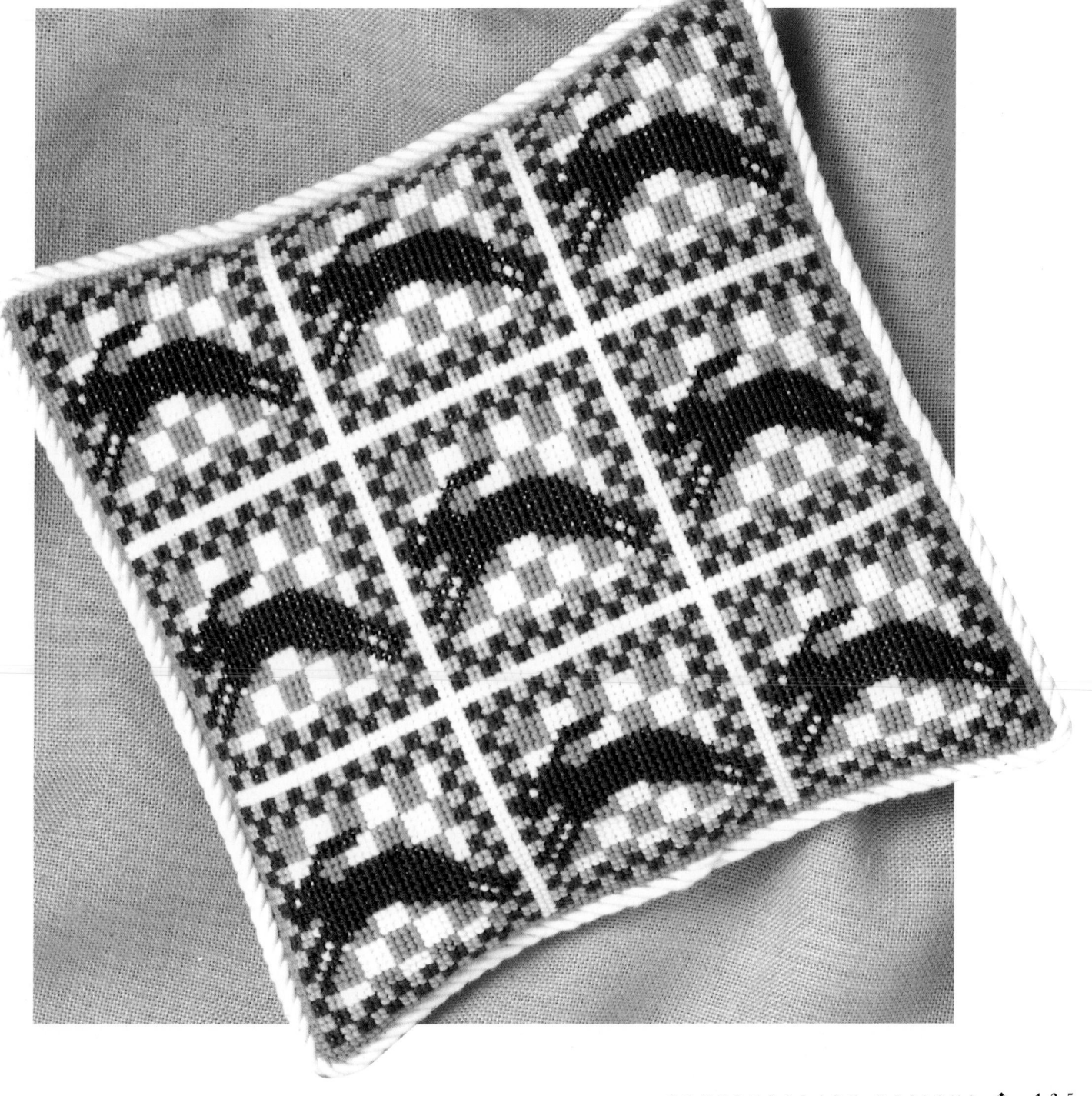

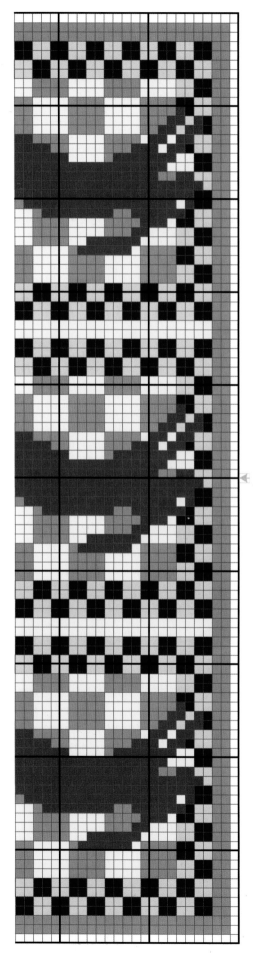

MATERIALS

❖ 16in (40cm) square of 7-count interlocking canvas, Anchor FSL075
❖ Appleton tapestry wool, four skeins each of 561, 563, 567, 967, 991
❖ size 16 tapestry needle
❖ large map pins
❖ plywood board
❖ scissors
❖ 18 x 26in (46 x 66cm) heavy-weight cream fabric
❖ sewing thread
❖ needle
❖ 1⅔ yds (1.5m) cream flanged cord
❖ 14in (36cm) cushion pad

TO STITCH

1 Fold the canvas in four to find the centre point and work the cross stitch using a single thickness of tapestry wool. Use at most a 20in (50cm) length of wool as a longer length may begin to thin towards the end and give poor coverage of the canvas. The canvas can be stitched with or without a frame. Unlike needlepoint which tends to pull the canvas diagonally, cross stitched canvas remains square.

2 Once the design is complete, it needs to be 'blocked' to even out the stitches and remove any creases from the canvas. To do this, follow the detailed instructions on page 28. Pin the canvas on top of the board, stretching it slightly as you go. Spray the cross stitch lightly with water until it is slightly damp and allow to dry away from direct heat.

TO MAKE UP

1 Turn under and stitch a 1in (2.5cm) hem across each short end of the cream fabric. Cut the panel in half crossways. Overlap the hems with the fabric right side up to make an 18in (46cm) square and tack together.

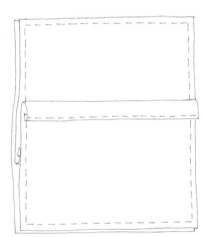

2 Pin and tack the flanged cord round the edge of the canvas with the cloth edging facing out and overlap the ends (see page 31). With right sides together, pin the cushion back to the canvas. Tack and machine round the edge of the canvas using a zipper foot.

3 Give the fabric back a final press, then trim across the corners and turn through. Insert the cushion pad to complete.

CROSS STITCH KEY

Appleton tapestry wool

■ Appleton 567
■ Appleton 967
▨ Appleton 561
▨ Appleton 563
□ Appleton 991

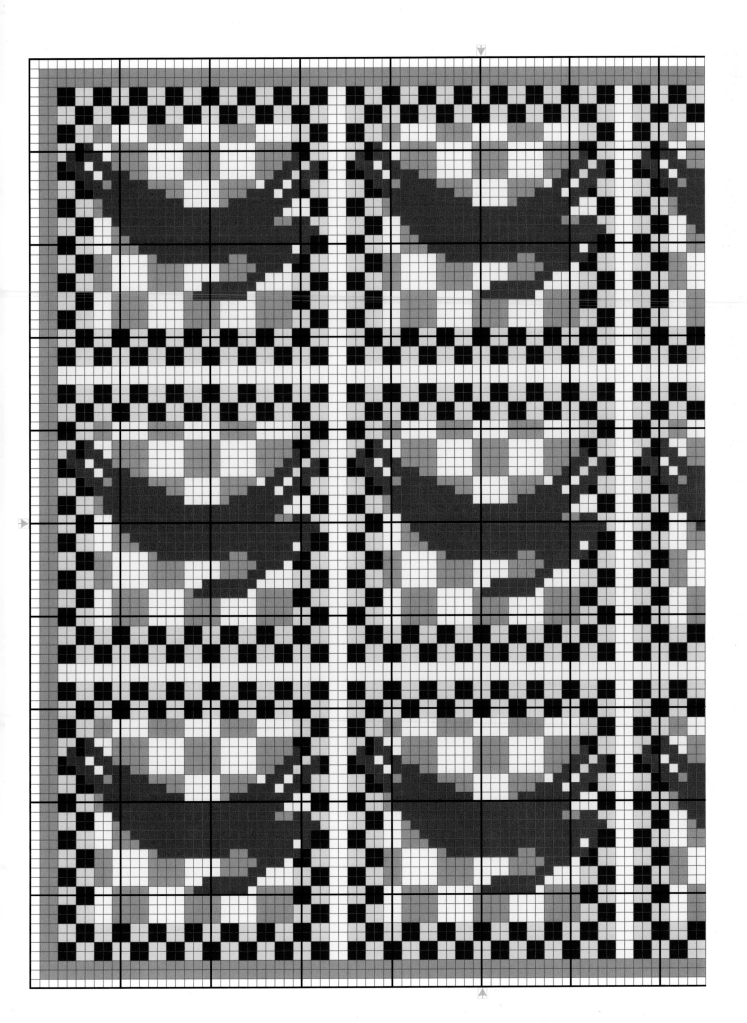

INDEX